# Recreational Ritalin
## The Not-So-Smart Drug

# ILLICIT AND MISUSED DRUGS

# ILLICIT AND MISUSED DRUGS

## Recreational Ritalin
# The Not-So-Smart Drug

*by Ida Walker*

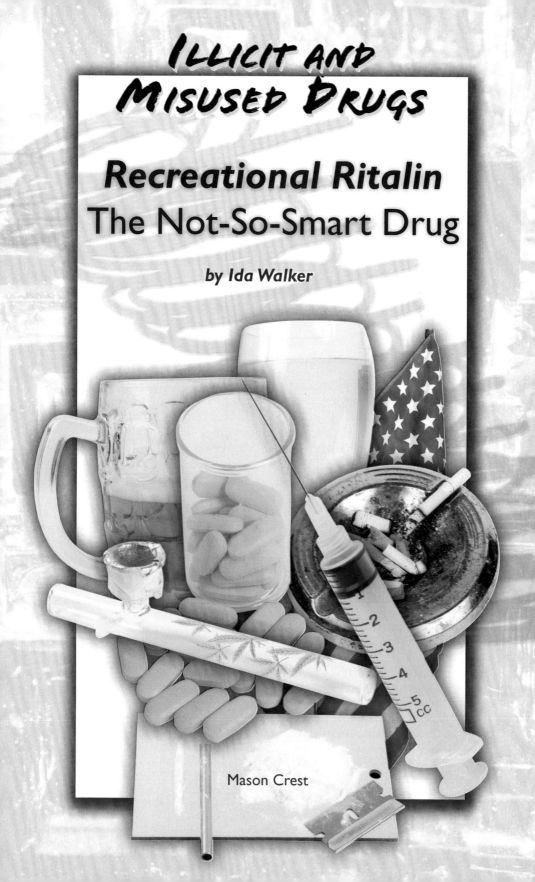

Mason Crest

Mason Crest
370 Reed Road
Broomall, Pennsylvania 19008
www.masoncrest.com

Printed in the Hashemite Kingdom of Jordan.

First printing
9 8 7 6 5 4 3 2 1

Library of Congress Cataloging-in-Publication Data

Walker, Ida.
Recreational ritalin : the not-so-smart drug / Ida Walker.
    p. cm. — (Illicit and misused drugs)
Includes bibliographical references and index.
ISBN 978-1-4222-2439-7 (hardcover)
ISBN 978-1-4222-2424-3 (series hardcover)
ISBN 978-1-4222-9303-4 (ebook)
1. Methylphenidate hydrochloride. 2. Attention-deficit hyperactivity disorder—Chemotherapy. 3. Medication abuse. 4. Teenagers—Drug use. 5. Children—Drug use. I. Title.
RJ506.H9W35 2012
616.85'89061—dc23
                                    2011032592

Interior design by Benjamin Stewart.
Cover design by Torque Advertising + Design.
Produced by Harding House Publishing Services, Inc.
www.hardinghousepages.com

# CONTENTS

## INTRODUCTION

Addicting drugs are among the greatest challenges to health, well-being, and the sense of independence and freedom for which we all strive—and yet these drugs are present in the everyday lives of most people. Almost every home has alcohol or tobacco waiting to be used, and has medicine cabinets stocked with possibly outdated but still potentially deadly drugs. Almost everyone has a friend or loved one with an addiction-related problem. Almost everyone seems to have a solution neatly summarized by word or phrase: medicalization, legalization, criminalization, war-on-drugs.

For better and for worse, drug information seems to be everywhere, but what information sources can you trust? How do you separate misinformation (whether deliberate or born of ignorance and prejudice) from the facts? Are prescription drugs safer than "street" drugs? Is occasional drug use really harmful? Is cigarette smoking more addictive than heroin? Is marijuana safer than alcohol? Are the harms caused by drug use limited to the users? Can some people become addicted following just a few exposures? Is treatment or counseling just for those with serious addiction problems?

These are just a few of the many questions addressed in this series. It is an empowering series because it provides the information and perspectives that can help people come to their own opinions and find answers to the challenges posed by drugs in their own lives. The series also provides further resources for information and assistance, recognizing that no single source has all the answers. It should be of interest and relevance to areas of study spanning biology, chemistry, history, health, social studies and more. Its efforts to provide a real-world context for the information that is clearly presented but not overly simplified should be appreciated by students, teachers, and parents.

The series is especially commendable in that it does not pretend to pose easy answers or imply that all decisions can be made on the basis of simple facts: some challenges have no immediate or simple solutions, and some solutions will need to rely as much upon basic values as basic facts. Despite this, the series should help to at least provide a foundation of knowledge. In the end, it may help as much by pointing out where the solutions are not simple, obvious, or known to work. In fact, at many points, the reader is challenged to think for him- or herself by being asked what his or her opinion is.

A core concept of the series is to recognize that we will never have all the facts, and many of the decisions will never be easy. Hopefully, however, armed with information, perspective, and resources, readers will be better prepared for taking on the challenges posed by addictive drugs in everyday life.

— *Jack E. Henningfield, Ph.D.*

# 1 What Is Ritalin?

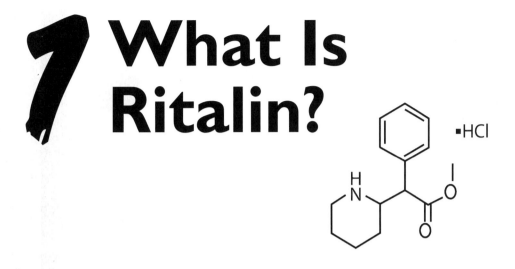

•HCl

Jason was a wiggle-worm even when he was a baby. "He never stopped kicking and moving," his mother said. "He seldom slept more than two hours at a time, and he cried a lot whenever I wasn't carrying him. He just seemed restless all the time."

Things seemed to get better when Jason became a toddler; he was constantly into mischief, but his parents expected that from a little boy. Keeping up with him kept them on their toes, but he was an affectionate and happy child. When he went to nursery school, however, his teachers complained about his behavior. "They thought he was an undisciplined child," his mother said, "but I knew it wasn't a discipline problem. He was just active. He couldn't sit still. And he got bored easily. He did better at home where it didn't matter if he ran and yelled all day."

Eventually, of course, Jason had to go to school—but he just couldn't seem to learn to sit quietly in his seat. He forgot to raise his hand before he talked, he didn't know how to use an "indoor voice," and he seemed incapable of staying in his seat. All day long, he wandered around the classroom and poked and tapped and chattered until he drove his teacher crazy.

Things didn't get any better as he got older; if anything, as more was expected from the other students in the classroom, Jason's behavior seemed worse by comparison. His teachers sent him to the principal's office; they

Children with ADHD have trouble sitting still and following directions. As a result, school is a challenge that gets harder every year.

## Brand Name vs. Generic Name

Talking about medications can be confusing because every drug has at least two names: its "generic name" and the "brand name" that the pharmaceutical company uses to market the drug. Generic names are based on the drug's chemical structure, while drug companies use brand names in order to inspire public recognition and loyalty for their products.

wrote notes home to his parents; they withheld privileges from him—but nothing seemed to work. Jason simply couldn't sit still and he couldn't be quiet. His parents were convinced he was a bright kid—but his grades told a different story. Homework bored Jason; so did tests; and so did paying attention in class. "Trying to get Jason to succeed in school," said his mother, "was like trying to fit a square peg in a round hole. He just didn't fit."

We've all known kids like Jason, individuals who can't sit still or pay attention for very long periods. They fidget, they interrupt, they run around. For them, school is an ordeal. For these students—those with attention-deficit/hyperactivity disorder (ADHD; formerly designated attention deficit disorder [ADD])—school can be a source of endless frustration, no matter how much they want to learn.

But for someone with ADHD, problems extend far beyond the classroom and long after childhood. They may have a hard time making friends, both as children and as adults. Grown-ups with ADHD may find their difficulty concentrating on projects can *compromise* their work situations.

For many with ADHD, however, there is help in the form of a drug patented in 1954.

## The History of Methylphenidate

In 1944, researchers looking for an effective treatment for depression, **chronic** fatigue, and **narcolepsy** first synthesized methylphenidate. Ten years later, the pharmaceutical company Ciba **patented** the medication for use in treating those conditions (among others). The drug was marketed under the brand name Ritalin®. Today, Ritalin is sold by Novartis and is available in pill or tablet form. Methylphenidate is also available under other names, such as Metadate®, Concerta®, and Methylin®. It is the most-often prescribed medication for the treatment of ADHD. Most Ritalin is produced in the United States, although

## Drug Approval

Before a drug can be marketed in the United States, it must be officially approved by the Food and Drug Administration (FDA). Today's FDA is the primary consumer protection agency in the United States. Operating under the authority given it by the government, and guided by laws established throughout the twentieth century, the FDA has established a rigorous drug approval process that verifies the safety, effectiveness, and accuracy of labeling for any drug marketed in the United States.

While the United States has the FDA for the approval and regulation of drugs and medical devices, Canada has a similar organization called the Therapeutic Product Directorate (TPD). The TPD is a division of Health Canada, the Canadian government's department of health. The TPD regulates drugs, medical devices, disinfectants, and sanitizers with disinfectant claims. Some of the things that the TPD monitors are quality, effectiveness, and safety. Just as the FDA must approve new drugs in the United States, the TPD must approve new drugs in Canada before those drugs can enter the market.

*A person with ADHD may feel like a square peg trying to fit into a round hole. A medication like Ritalin is supposed to help him fit in a little better.*

some methylphenidate products are made in Mexico and Argentina for companies other than Novartis. Ritalin and other forms of methylphenidate are used in Europe as well as the United States, though the United States is the number-one user of the drug.

Ritalin has been used to treat a multitude of conditions since it received approval from the U.S. Food and Drug Administration (FDA). In 1957, the **Physicians' Desk Reference** described it as being "indicated in chronic fatigue and depressed states, including those associated with tranquilizing agents and other drugs; disturbed senile behavior; **psychoneuroses** and psychoses associated with depression; and in narcolepsy." In the 1960s, health-care professionals began prescribing Ritalin for children with hyperactivity or minimal brain dysfunction; today, those children would be diagnosed as having ADHD.

Ritalin replaced other drugs, such as benzedrine, in the treatment of hyperactivity. *Off-label uses* of Ritalin include prescriptions for poststroke patients, the elderly with depression, and cancer patients.

## How Ritalin Works

Ritalin and the other methylphenidates stimulate the central nervous system (CNS) by affecting the release and uptake of dopamine, a neurotransmitter. Neurotransmitters are chemicals that play an integral role in the brain's complex communication system. The basic unit of this messenger system is the neuron, or nerve cell. Messages are carried to the brain by presynaptic—sending—neurons. An electrical impulse is sent down the neuron's long, whip-like tail (axon) to the terminal buttons at its end. The neurons do not touch each other, so when the impulse reaches the terminal buttons, it hitches a ride with the neurotransmitters across the synapse, the gap between the neurons, until it reaches its destination, the dendrites (root-looking projections) of the receiving—postsynaptic—neuron. With successful delivery, communication takes place, and an action is performed.

### Fast Fact

Presynaptic neurons are the senders and carry the message as far as the synapse; their action occurs before (pre) the message reaches the synapse.

Postsynaptic neurons take delivery of the message after (post) it leaves the synapse.

Presynaptic neurons carefully monitor how much neurotransmitter they release. In order to maintain an adequate supply, they may reuptake some of the neurotransmitters floating in the synapse. The dendrites of the postsynaptic neuron pick up other neurotransmitters to complete the communication process.

Ritalin works to block the reuptake of the neurotransmitter dopamine, making more of it available in the brain. The dopamine stimulates the brain's frontal lobes, limbic system, and cortex, thereby activating the brain's behavior-control centers. The frontal lobes are responsible for concentration, decision making, planning, learning and retention, and helping a person behave in an appropriate manner in a given situation. The cortex keeps individuals "in check." A properly functioning cortex helps to keep individuals from being hyperactive, helps control anger, and inhibits behaviors such as saying inappropriate things. Emotions are controlled by the

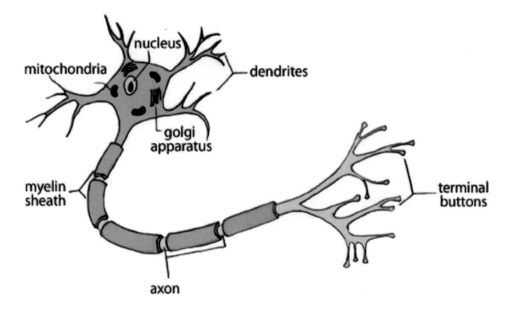

*Ritalin stimulates the central nervous system, by targeting dopamine, a neurotransmitter. Neurotransmitters carry messages between nerve cells.*

limbic system. If the limbic system is overstimulated, extreme mood swings might occur. A hypersensitive **startle response** can also be evident as well as disrupted sleep patterns. The ability to cope with stress may be affected by an overstimulated limbic system. Ritalin helps to even out all these complicated systems in the person with ADHD.

## Contraindications and Warnings

Like most drugs, there are some people for whom the drug is **contraindicated**. According to the website www.mentalhealth.org, among those who should *not* take Ritalin are people with

- anxiety
- tension
- agitation
- *thyrotoxicosis*
- *tachyarrhythmias*
- severe *angina*
- *glaucoma*

It is also not recommended for people with **motor tics** or a family history of **Tourette's syndrome**.

There is a potential for abuse and dependence with the use of methylphenidate, and anyone who might be predisposed to addiction and dependence should not be prescribed the medication. Because of the drug's potential for abuse, the U.S. Department of Justice, Drug Enforcement Agency (DEA) lists it as a Schedule II controlled substance. Anyone who is caught and found guilty of dealing Ritalin faces stiff penalties.

Other drugs can affect how Ritalin works in the body. It should not be taken if a **monoamine oxidase inhibitor**

*Ritalin was first synthesized in 1944 in an attempt to find an effective treatment for abnormal sleepiness and tiredness.*

**(MAOI)**, phenelzine, or tranylcypromine was taken during the past two weeks. According to the website www.drug.com, the health-care provider should be told if the patient is taking any of the following, as dosage adjustments or special monitoring will need to take place:

- warfarin
- phenytoin
- phenobarbital
- primidone
- a tricyclic antidepressant
- a selective serotonin reuptake inhibitor
- guanethidine

## U.S. Department of Justice Drug Enforcement Agency Drug Schedule

Schedule I
- The drug or other substance has a high potential for abuse.
- The drug or other substance has no currently accepted medical use in treatment in the United States.
- There is a lack of accepted safety for use of the drug or other substance under medical supervision.
- Some Schedule I substances are heroin, LSD, and marijuana.

Schedule II
- The drug or other substance has a high potential for abuse.
- The drug or other substance has a currently accepted medical use in treatment in the United States or a currently accepted medical use with severe restrictions.
- Abuse of the drug or other substance may lead to severe psychological or physical dependence.
- Schedule II substances include morphine, PCP, cocaine, methadone, and methamphetamine.

Schedule III
- The drug or other substance has a potential for abuse less than the drugs or other substances in Schedules I and II.
- The drug or other substance has a currently accepted medical use in treatment in the United States.
- Abuse of the drug or other substance may lead to moderate or low physical dependence or high psychological dependence.
- Anabolic steroids, codeine, and hydrocodone with aspirin or Tylenol, and some barbiturates are Schedule III substances.

Schedule IV
- The drug or other substance has a low potential for abuse relative to the drugs or other substances in Schedule III.
- The drug or other substance has a currently accepted medical use in treatment in the United States.
- Abuse of the drug or other substance may lead to limited physical dependence or psychological dependence relative to the drugs or other substances in Schedule III.
- Included in Schedule IV are Darvon, Talwin, Equanil, Valium, and Xanax.

Schedule V
- The drug or other substance has a low potential for abuse relative to the drugs or other substances in Schedule IV.
- The drug or other substance has a currently accepted medical use in treatment in the United States.
- Abuse of the drug or other substance may lead to limited physical dependence or psychological dependence relative to the drugs or other substances in Schedule IV.
- Over-the-counter cough medicines with codeine are classified in Schedule V.

(*Source:* www.dea.gov.)

## Ritalin's Short-Term and Long-Term Side Effects

Like many medications, methylphenidate—Ritalin—has both potential short-term and long-term side effects. In the short term, individuals taking Ritalin may experience nervousness and insomnia, loss of appetite, nausea and vomiting, dizziness, heart *palpitations*, headaches, arrhythmias, increased blood pressure, skin rashes and itching, abdominal pain and cramping, weight loss, digestive problems, and psychotic episodes. In rare cases, *toxic psychosis* may develop. An individual may experience depression when stopping the medication.

Potential side effects of long-term use include loss of appetite that could lead to malnutrition, tremors and muscle twitching, fever, convulsions, headaches (including severe migraines), potentially life-threatening arrhythmias and respiratory problems, anxiety, restlessness, paranoia, hallucinations, delusions, excessive repetition of movements and meaningless tasks, and *formication*.

Ritalin helps to treat many children with ADHD, but its use remains controversial. In part, this is because it has many potential side effects as well as a high potential for abuse.

These side effects don't occur with every patient. It is up to that patient, the patient's family, and the health-care professional to determine if the real benefits of taking the medication outweigh the potential drawbacks.

As more kids are diagnosed with ADHD, parents and professionals look for better ways to help these kids cope with their condition. Ritalin is one of the most common and most successful treatments for ADHD. Despite this, its use remains controversial for a variety of reasons. But then, so is the condition it's most often prescribed to treat.

# 2 Attention-Deficit Hyperactivity Disorder

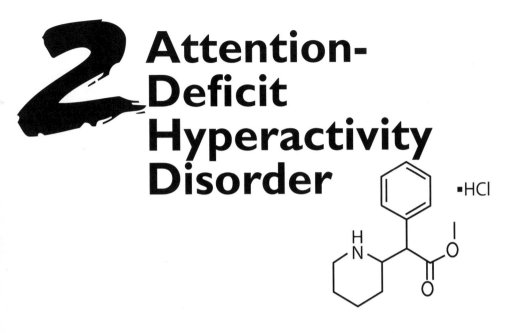

•HCl

At nine years of age, Jake is already starting to avoid school. His teacher reports that he squirms around in his seat, stands up unexpectedly, and seldom finishes his work. The kids sitting near him in class say he's always interrupting and shouting out the answers (generally wrong). His desk is a mess; papers are on the floor and his work is disorganized. He's often picked last for games, and then he tries to spoil the game for the others.

Sarah, age fourteen, chooses to sit in the back of the classroom, and much of the time she's doodling in her notebook or staring out of the window. She seldom completes assignments and often forgets to bring the right books to class. Her locker is a jumbled mass of papers and books, and she usually can't find what she's looking for. Much of the time, she feels resentful and says that everybody picks on her.

Danny, age four, attends preschool. He has an aide assigned specifically to help him comply with the routine of the group, but he would prefer to roam around the room, picking up toys here and there. Whatever activity in which the rest of his group is engaged seldom engages him for long. During story time, he doesn't become involved in the story, but keeps repeating the same questions in a loud tone of voice. Danny's mother states that she avoids family gatherings and celebrations because he gets overly excited and then she can't control him. (Source: NYU Child Study Center. www. aboutourkids.org/aboutour/articles/about_adhd. html.)

These are real kids with real problems. They have been diagnosed with attention-deficit/hyperactivity disorder —ADHD. Some people think this is a relatively new disorder; after all, you never used to hear this term, but now it's in the news a lot. Actually, however, ADHD has a long history.

## History of ADHD

Written references to an ADHD-like condition can be traced back to nineteenth-century Germany. In 1845, Heinrich Hoffmann was a physician and the author of numerous books on medicine and psychiatry as well as poetry. The father of a three-year-old son, he was frustrated when he couldn't find appropriate reading materi-

*When she should be sitting, the child with ADHD is likely to be wandering around the classroom.*

als for the little boy. He turned to his talents as a poet and wrote a book of poems titled *Der Struwwelpeter*, which has been translated into thirty languages (the American author Mark Twain is responsible for one of the best-known English translations). Called *Fidgety Philip* in English, the poem tells the story of a little boy whose behavior drives his parents wild.

"Let me see if Philip can
Be a little gentleman;
Let me see if he is able
To sit still for once at table."

Thus spoke, in earnest tone,
The father to his son;
And the mother looked very grave
To see Philip so misbehave.
But Philip he did not mind
His father who was so kind.
He wriggled
And giggled,
And then, I declare,
Swung backward and forward
And tilted his chair,
Just like any rocking horse;—
"Philip! I am getting cross!"
See the naughty, restless child,
Growing still more rude and wild ,
Till his chair falls over quite.
Philip screams with all his might,
Catches at the cloth, but then
That makes matters worse again.
Down upon the ground they fall,
Glasses, bread, knives forks and all.
How Mamma did fret and frown,
When she saw them tumbling down!
And Papa made such a face!
Philip is in sad disgrace.
Where is Philip? Where is he?
Fairly cover'd up, you see!
Cloth and all are lying on him;
He has pull'd down all upon him!
What a terrible to-do!
 Dishes, glasses, snapt in two!
Here a knife, and there a fork!
Philip, this is naughty work.

Table all so bare, and ah!
Poor Papa and poor Mamma
Look quite cross, and wonder how
They shall make their dinner now.

*In 1845 Heinrich Hoffman wrote about Der Struwwelpeter, which translates to "Shockheaded Peter." In the stories, Peter is a trouble-maker, who today might be diagnosed with ADHD.*

## Nature vs. Nurture

For many years there has been a discussion in the scientific community about what is important in the development of physical and behavioral traits—nature or nurture.

Nature refers to inherited qualities, thereby free from outside influences. To those who believe that nature is the overriding factor, we are who we are genetically; there's nothing we (or anyone else) can do about it.

Historically, the nurture argument referred primarily to the care given by the parents or other primary caregiver. Today, childhood friends, television, and even prenatal experiences are included in the nurture side of the debate.

Today, scientists realize that "nurture" and "nature" cannot be separated; physical characteristics (nature) may make an individual more susceptible to environmental challenges (nurture). The two things interact, each shaping the other.

Today Philip might be diagnosed as having ADHD. Children with this condition are often the Dennis-the-Menaces of the world, children who are constantly into mischief, who can't sit still, who learn to run before they ever learn to walk. In the world of Winnie the Pooh, Tigger would be the one with ADHD, bouncing through life before he thinks through the consequences of his actions. Children's literature makes clear that people were well acquainted with this type of children long before there was a "scientific" name for their condition.

In 1890, American psychologist William James described a personality trait, "the explosive will," that was defined as the opposing condition to attentiveness. It wouldn't be until the twentieth century, however, that ADHD would be officially "discovered." In 1902, George F. Still, an English pediatrician, delivered a series of lectures to the Royal College of Physicians. In the lectures,

Parents' influence and other environmental factors are important in a child's life, but genetics may have more to do with ADHD than parenting techniques.

## Recreational Ritalin—The Not-So-Smart Drug 29

ADHD refers to a *group* of behaviors, not just one. Included under the classification of ADHD are:

- hyperactivity
- impulsivity
- attention problems

Signs of Inattention

- becoming easily distracted by irrelevant sights and sounds
- failing to pay attention to details and making careless mistakes
- rarely following instructions carefully and completely
- losing or forgetting things like toys, pencils, or books

Signs of Hyperactivity and Impulsivity

- squirming or fidgeting with hands or feet
- running, climbing, or leaving seat where quiet behavior is expected
- blurting out answers before hearing the whole question
- having difficulty waiting in line or taking turns

he described a group of children who had problems with impulse control and behavior. Still initially described these behaviors as being "a defect of moral control." But, he did not blame poor parenting—nurturing—for the children's ill behaviors. Still believed the hyperactive behaviors were caused by a genetic factor—nature.

Medical treatments for these behaviors were first noted in 1937, when doctors found that **amphetamines** reduced hyperactive and **impulsive** behaviors. In the mid-1950s, methylphenidate (Ritalin) was also discovered to be effective in the treatment of these disorders.

The term "hyperactive child syndrome" was not used until the 1960s, when researcher Stella Chase first used it. At the time, many physicians and researchers still blamed bad parenting for hyperactive and impulsive behaviors. Chase, however, believed the disorder had a strong biological component. During the 1960s, use of **stimulants** to treat the condition became widespread.

In 1980, the American Psychiatric Association (APA) classified a collection of behavior patterns as Attention Deficit Disorder without Hyperactivity (ADD) and Attention-Deficit Disorder with Hyperactivity (ADHD).

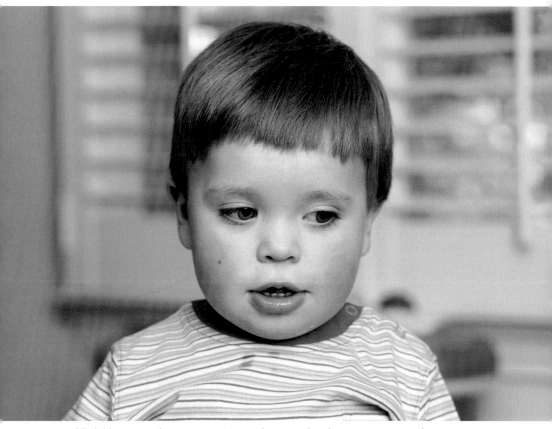

*All children seem hyperactive at times, because they have more energy than adults, and have more trouble focusing on tasks. ADHD becomes a possibility only if a child shows these behaviors a lot more than his peers.*

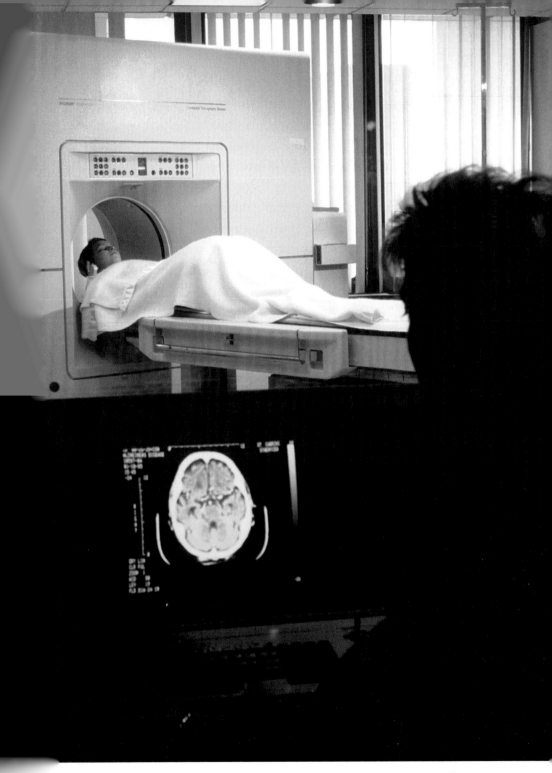

*Researchers use CAT scans to study the brains of individuals with ADHD. This has allowed researchers to determine that ADHD may be caused by a developmental failure in the brain's circuitry.*

# Chapter 2—Attention-Deficit Hyperactivity Disorder

Seven years later, ADD was included as part of ADHD. The APA classified it as a medical condition with behavioral problems that differ from those caused by stressors such as divorce, a death in the family, or changing schools. In other words, parents are not to blame for a child's ADHD.

In the book *Attention-Deficit Hyperactivity Disorder*, Dr. Russell Barkley looks at ADHD in terms of two sets of symptoms: inattention and a combination of hyperactive and impulsive behaviors. "Most children are more active, distractible, and impulsive than adults," he acknowledges. "And they are more inconsistent, affected by momentary events and dominated by objects in their immediate environment. The younger the children, the less able they are to be aware of time or to give priority to future events over more immediate wants. Such behaviors are signs of problems, however, when children display them significantly more than their peers do."

## Causes of ADHD

Even though most in the scientific community now acknowledge that ADHD has a biological component, there is still much that is not understood about its causes. No single cause of ADHD has been determined.

### Brain Activity and ADHD

Developments in technology have aided researchers in the study of the brain and how it works. Computer-aided tomography (CAT) scans, positron emission tomography (PET) scans, and magnetic resonance imaging (MRI) have allowed doctors to study the brains of individuals diagnosed with ADHD without performing invasive procedures.

For years researchers assumed that ADHD was caused by an inability of the brain to filter out competing sensory input; in other words, a child with this problem would be constantly distracted by sights and sounds because of neurological impairment. However, recent research shows that ADHD is not a disorder of attention so much as it is a developmental failure in the brain circuitry that underlies inhibition and self-control. This means that children with ADHD cannot control their *responses* to sensory input.

In other words, individuals diagnosed with ADHD are unable to control their reactions to sensory stimulation. If their surroundings bring an idea to their attention, they are very apt to act on it, regardless of the consequences. For instance, one child with ADHD put a worm in his mouth and swallowed it; another, while pretending to be Superman, jumped out of a tree and broke his arm; and yet another blasted his little sister's hair with red spray paint. All of these behaviors might have occurred to another child, but most children have the self-control necessary to refrain from acting on every idea that pops into their heads.

Other researchers, Dr. Barkley says, have found that these children are less capable of thinking ahead, preparing their actions in anticipation of upcoming events. They also fail to slow down to improve their accuracy at a task, even though they have been given feedback that they are making mistakes. One study found that brain-wave activity was extremely slow in children diagnosed with ADHD compared to those without the disorder. This indicates a lack of control in the cortex, one of the inhibitory parts of the brain (see chapter 1).

Although a direct causal connection has not been established, researchers have discovered that some areas of

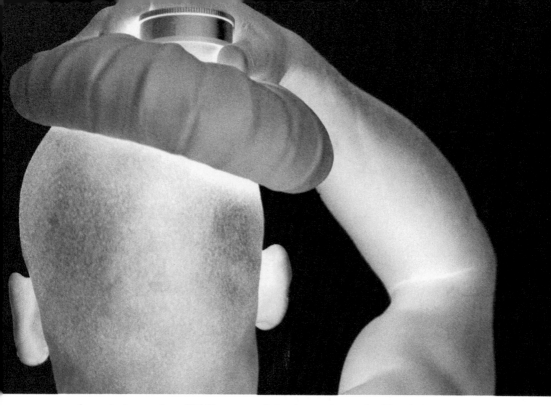

An early theory about ADHD suggested that it was the result of head injuries. However, researchers now think that head injuries account for a very small percentage of ADHD cases.

the brain are about 5 to 10 percent smaller and less active in children diagnosed with ADHD. No one has been able to determine why these specific parts of the brain are smaller, but some researchers believe gene *mutations*, such as those caused by drug and alcohol abuse during pregnancy, heredity, or exposure to toxins either before birth or after, may be the culprits.

As researchers learn more about the inner workings of the brain, they have been able to advance some theories behind the development of ADHD and discard others.

## Head Injuries

One of the first theories surrounding the development of ADHD was that it was caused by head injuries that led to brain damage. Most research has determined that, at

*Researchers have found evidence of underlying genetic factors that lead to the development of ADHD. For example, in twin studies, if one twin is diagnosed with ADHD, there is a 55-92% chance that the other will be as well.*

most, head injuries may account for a very small percentage of ADHD diagnoses.

## Genetics and Biology

ADHD frequently occurs multiple times within families, leading most authorities to believe the disorder has a genetic link. According to the National Institute of Mental Health (NIMH), studies have shown that 25 percent of the close relatives of the families of children diagnosed with ADHD also have ADHD; only 5 percent of the general population has the disorder. *Twin studies* have also shown a genetic link to ADHD; one study showed that between 55 and 92 percent of identical twins of individuals with ADHD will eventually be diagnosed with it as well. Another large study of twins by Helene Gjone and Jon M. Sundet found that ADHD has a heritability of close to 80 percent; in other words, up to 80 percent of the differences in attention, hyperactivity, and impulsivity between people with ADHD and those without can be explained by genetic factors. The Attention-Deficit Hyperactivity Disorder Molecular Genetics Network, established in 1999, operates as a *clearinghouse* for researchers on the genetic influences of ADHD. Many of these researchers believe that the defective genes are the ones that tell dopamine how to carry messages from one nerve cell to another. This means that the children who have these defective genes will have less self-control over their own behavior.

## Environmental Influences

The effect of the environment on biology is a rapidly growing area of concern among researchers of many physical conditions. For example, some scientists believe

*Genetics are just one factor in the development of ADHD; environment also plays a role. Some researchers point to the artificial flavorings and colorings in food and drinks as a contributing cause.*

there is a connection between thimerosal (a derivative of mercury) present in some vaccines and the occurrence of autism. Many ADHD researchers also believe there is a relationship between the environment and ADHD. The NIMH reports that some studies have shown a relationship between the mother's use of cigarettes and alcohol during pregnancy and the development of ADHD.

Another area of concern for these researchers is the high level of lead in the blood of preschool children. Some researchers believe there is a connection between the levels of lead in the body and ADHD. The most common source of lead is from paint, though it is believed that children living in congested urban areas can also be exposed to lead from various forms of air pollution and from the lead contained in many old plumbing pipes. Lead paint has been outlawed in the United States since the 1970s. However, many older buildings still have lead-based paints and lead plumbing. In many cases, affected children are living in poverty and least likely to receive extra services that might be needed to be able to function well as someone living with ADHD.

### Food Additives

Refined sugar and other food additives have also been suggested as possible causes of ADHD. Those who believe that these play a prominent role encourage the elimination of anything containing artificial ingredients (especially flavorings and colorings), preservatives, and all forms of sugar from the diets of children who have exhibited hyperactive or inattentive behaviors. However, the scientific community has not supported this theory. The NIMH reports that a study in 1982 found that such restrictions helped only 5 percent of children with ADHD, primarily young children and those who were diagnosed with food allergies.

Together, environmental factors may explain from 20 to 30 percent of ADHD cases among boys, and an even smaller percentage among girls. This means that most cases of ADHD are linked to genetic inheritance.

### Symptoms and Diagnosis of ADHD

Lisa's son Jack had always been a handful. Even as a preschooler, he would tear through the house like a tornado, shouting, roughhousing, and climbing the furniture. No toy or activity ever held his interest for more than a few minutes, and he would dart off without warning, seemingly unaware of the dangers of a busy street or a crowded mall.

It was exhausting to parent Jack, but Lisa hadn't been too concerned back then. He'll grow out of it, she figured. But here he was, now eight, and still no easier to handle.

**Individuals diagnosed as having ADHD may also have other conditions that will affect their learning skills:**

Dyslexia: specific problems with written language—the transposition of letters and numbers, for example.

Dyspraxia: problems planning and executing movements; poor motor coordination and inattention.

Every day it was a struggle to get Jack to settle down long enough to complete even the simplest tasks, from chores to homework. When his teacher's comments about his inattention and disruptive behavior in class became too frequent to ignore, Lisa took Jack to the doctor, who recommended an evaluation for attention deficit hyperactivity disorder (ADHD).

As Lisa found with her son, whose story is told on the Web site kidshealth.org, ADHD symptoms generally appear while the child is young. They usually do not appear all at once, occurring instead over a course of months. First to appear are symptoms related to impulsiveness and hyperactivity; impaired attention symptoms come later. According to the *Diagnostic and Statistical Manual of Mental Disorders, Fourth Edition, Revised* (DSM-IV-R), ADHD is a "pattern of inattention and/or hyperactivity and impulsivity that is more frequently displayed and more severe than is typically observed in individuals at a comparable level of development." These characteristics must also:

- cause some kind of impairment before the age of seven

A parent who thinks her child might have ADHD should talk to the family doctor. The doctor can help with a diagnosis and make suggestions for treatment.

**Recreational Ritalin—The Not-So-Smart Drug** 41

- be present in at least two settings (for example, school, work, and home)
- show evidence of interfering with developmentally appropriate functioning at work, school, or in social situations
- must not be explained by other physical or psychological conditions

The DSM-IV-R divides ADHD into three behavior patterns: predominately hyperactive-impulsive type, in which inattention does not play a major role; predominately inattentive type, in which hyperactivity and impulsiveness are not major factors; and combined type, in which characteristics of the other types are evident.

Each type of ADHD has specific characteristics. Symptoms of the hyperactive-impulsivity type are:

- feeling restless, fidgeting, or squirming while seated
- running, climbing, or leaving a seat when and where it is inappropriate
- blurting out answers before a question is completed
- finding it difficult to wait in line or to take turns

Symptoms of ADHD inattention type include:

- being easily distracted by irrelevant sights and sounds
- failing to pay attention and making careless mistakes
- following instructions carelessly and incompletely or forgetting items like toys, pencils, books, and tools needed to complete a task
- skipping from one incomplete task to another

A child who exhibits *some* of these behaviors is not necessarily exhibiting ADHD. He could be simply be immature for his age. When making a diagnosis of ADHD, doctors look for *patterns* of behavior, not isolated incidents. She will also compare the child's behaviors with those of other children the same chronological age and at the same developmental level.

A parent who suspects her child might have ADHD should consult a qualified health-care professional for a diagnosis. The doctor or other health-care professional will first eliminate anything that might produce symptoms that mimic ADHD, including:

- a stressor in the child's life (such as a divorce or death in the family)
- undetected seizures
- middle ear infection that can cause hearing loss
- a learning disability
- anxiety or depression

Once other potential causes of the behavior are ruled out, the individual will undergo a battery of tests, including intelligence and learning and achievement tests.

The earlier a child is diagnosed as having ADHD, the sooner strategies for handling the problems that can come with the disorder can be put into place. One of the hardest places for someone diagnosed with ADHD to cope is school.

A study of 400 seven-year-olds found that 50 percent of those diagnosed with dyspraxia also had ADHD. According to the Dyslexia Research Institute, approximately 60 percent of children diagnosed with dyslexia also have ADHD.

ADHD, dyslexia, and dyspraxia have some common characteristics:

- neurodevelopmental anomalies including pregnancy and birth complications, low birth weight, small head circumference, and minor physical problems
- more males than females are affected
- allergies/autoimmune problems
- other physical ailments such as stomachaches and migraines
- problems with motor coordination
- problems with sleep patterns
- mood disorders such as depression or mood swings
- behavioral problems such as hostility, aggression when stressed, impulsivity, and hyperactivity
- perceptual and cognitive problems such as visual and auditory problems and attention/working memory difficulties

## ADHD at School

Think about it. Where do most kids spend most of their waking hours? At school. And school can be a very difficult place for a student diagnosed with ADHD. According to B. Jacqueline Stordy and Malcolm J. Nicholl, authors of *The LCP Solution: The Remarkable Nutritional Treatment for ADHD, Dyslexia, & Dyspraxia*, "about half of ADHD children repeat a grade by adolescence, 35 percent eventually drop out of school, and only 5 percent finish college."

Students diagnosed with ADHD are guaranteed assistance with their educational program under the National Rehabilitation Act, Section 504 (often referred to only as Section 504) and the Individuals with Disabilities

Education Act (IDEA). ADHD is considered a health impairment that affects the child's ability to learn and interact with others.

Passed in 1973, the National Rehabilitation Act and its Section 504 prohibits discrimination against people with disabilities. In 1975, Congress passed and the president signed into law the Education for the Handicapped Act, also called Public Law 94-142. When the law was reauthorized, it was renamed the Individuals with Disabilities Education Act (IDEA). This law gives states federal funds to serve the needs of people between the ages of three and twenty-one who have disabilities. A well-defined process is designed to ensure that all children

*Children with ADHD have a very difficult time in school. This only gets worse as the child get older, such that only 5% of individuals with ADHD graduate from college.*

A child with ADHD will need extra attention from parents, teachers and school psychologists to help him be successful in school. They will all have to work together to devise a plan specifically tailored to that child's needs.

have access to an "appropriate education" in the least restrictive environment possible.

Public Law 94-142 and the subsequent IDEA guarantees that every school in every educational system will:

1. *Search.* Each school will have a procedure in place to search for and identify students with a disability. Testing will be provided for those suspected of having one.
2. *Find.* When a student with a potential problem is identified, a system is in place for collecting information and designing an evaluation process.

3. *Evaluation.* A comprehensive and multidisciplinary evaluation shall be done and include the school psychologist, teachers, and other support personnel.
4. *Conference.* Once the evaluation is complete, the student's parents or guardians will meet with school personnel to discuss its results and propose plans for the child's educational program.
5. *Parents' decision process.* After the conference, the parents or guardians will decide whether to accept, request changes, or reject the plan as offered by the school.
6. *Appeals process.* If the parents reject the diagnosis, placement, or education plan, an appeals process starts with the local school and can then be appealed at the county or state level.
7. *Follow-up.* Families are provided progress reports and a formal reevaluation is done every three years, or sooner if requested.

An important part of an effective educational program for children diagnosed with ADHD and other disabilities

## How Prevalent Is ADHD?

The American Psychiatric Association estimates that between 3 and 7% of school-aged children have ADHD. Some studies suggest that rates of ADHD are much higher.

Although diagnosing ADHD in preschool children is difficult, estimates of the number involved in this age group are at 2 percent, and inattention is now a leading problem among young children.

is the Individualized Education Plan (IEP), provided for under IDEA. Working together, parents, teachers, school psychologists, and other support personnel devise a plan that outlines skills and learning activities the student needs to accomplish. Included in the IEP should be:

1. A statement of the child's current level of educational performance.
2. A statement of yearly goals or achievements expected for each area of identified weakness by the end of the school year.
3. Short-term objectives stated in instructional terms
4. A statement of the specific special education and support services to be provided to the student.
5. A statement of the extent to which a child will be able to participate in regular educational programs and justification for any special placement recommendations.
6. Projected dates for the beginning of services and how long they are anticipated to last.
7. A statement of the criteria and evaluation procedures to be used in determining whether the short-term objectives have been achieved; this should occur at least annually if not more often.

Through experience, parents and teachers have devised ways to make the school environment better for students diagnosed with ADHD. Authors Stordy

**FAST FACT**

Boys are more than twice as likely than girls to be diagnosed with ADHD.

## Stimulants Used in Treating ADHD

| Trade Name | Generic Name | Approved Age |
|---|---|---|
| Adderall* | amphetamine | 3 and older |
| Concerta | methylphenidate (long acting) | 6 and older |
| Cylert** | pemoline | 6 and older |
| Dexedrine | dextroamphetamine | 3 and older |
| Dextrostat | dextroamphetamine | 3 and older |
| Focalin | dexmethylphenidate | 6 and older |
| Metadate ER | methylphenidate (extended release) | 6 and older |
| Metadate CD | methylphenidate (extended release) | 6 and older |
| Ritalin | methylphenidate | 6 and older |
| Ritalin SR | methylphenidate (extended release) | 6 and older |
| Ritalin LA | methylphenidate (long acting) | 6 and older |

*Although Adderall is still available in the United States, Canada pulled a form of the drug, Adderall XR, from its market in 2005, citing deaths in Europe potentially connected to the drug.

**Because of its potential for serious side effects affecting the liver, Cylert should not ordinarily be considered as a first-line drug therapy for ADHD.

(*Source*: National Institute of Mental Health, *Attention Deficit Hyperactivity Disorder*, 2003.)

and Nicholl list some of these in their book *The LCP Solution*:

- Seat children with ADHD at the front of the class and away from distractions such as windows.
- Have students with ADHD sit near students who model good behavior and study skills.

- Schedule physical activities between times when it is necessary for students to sit at their desks.
- Make sure there are no unnecessary objects or materials on the student's desktop.
- Establish eye contact with the student before giving her instructions, and explain that you are about to give her instructions and she must pay attention.
- Give one instruction at a time, in as few words as possible.

*Parents and teachers need to learn how to help a child with ADHD fit into the school environment. A couple suggestions include keeping her desk away from a window and free of unnecessary items.*

## ADHD and the Perception of Time

Russell Barkley, one of today's leading experts on ADHD, has done experiments that look at the way kids with ADHD experience time. The results demonstrate how a basic problem with self-regulation can have far-reaching consequences.

In one experiment, Barkley turned on a light for a predetermined length of time and then asked a child to turn the light back on and off for what the child guessed to be the same interval. Children without ADHD performed fairly consistently. At twelve seconds, for example, their guesses were just a little low. At thirty-six seconds, they were slightly less accurate—still on the low side—and at sixty seconds their guesses were around fifty seconds. Kids with ADHD, however, were way off. At twelve seconds, they were well over the actual time; apparently, twelve seconds seemed much, much longer to them. At sixty seconds, though, their guesses were much lower; apparently, the longer interval was impossible for them to comprehend.

There are real-life consequences to having a sense of time that's off from everyone else's. For example, people with ADHD often have problems with punctuality and with patience. An accurate sense of time is necessary for comparing the duration of ongoing events with that of past events, so that a red light doesn't seem like an outrageous imposition, or five minutes doesn't seem like an impossibly long time to wait for a teacher's attention.

- Provide frequent feedback to help the student understand if he is on track.
- Provide opportunities to succeed.

But, school is not the only place where adjustments have to be made when there is someone in the family who has been diagnosed with ADHD. Home can also be a frustrating place for her and those around her. Parents, teachers, and other support persons have also come up with a list of suggestions for ways of making things run more smoothly at home:

- Establish incentives for good behavior and disincentives for negative behavior.
- Try to direct the child's energy toward sports—especially ones that require him to be in motion much of the time.
- Use calming background music to help the child focus on tasks at hand.
- Take books, tapes, and toys your child will need to remain occupied and amused while traveling.
- Keep shopping trips and errands brief. Be sure not to start out on these when your child is tired.

Just as important as making sure the child has an educational experience conducive to learning, parents of children diagnosed with ADHD must be aware of their treatment options. ADHD treatment plans are not one-size-fits-all.

## Treatment Options

### Medication

Although behavioral interventions are always tried first, the most common ADHD treatment is medication. Even there, parents have options depending on the needs of their child and any reactions that might have been caused by other medications. The most effective medications are stimulants, the most often-prescribed being Ritalin.

Although stimulants have proven to be the most effective medications for treating ADHD, other types of drugs have also been used. In some cases, antidepressants have been a treatment option. However, in 2004, the FDA warned that their use could lead to an increased risk of suicide for children and teenagers, although they believed that risk to be rare. Also in 2004, the FDA approved a nonstimulant drug for treating ADHD. Strattera, an **atomoxetine**, is not without controversy, however. Although it has been shown to be effective, the drug's manufacturer, Eli Lilly & Co., has issued an advisory warning against possible liver disease.

In April 2006, the FDA approved Daytrana, the first **transdermal** patch for the treatment of ADHD in children between the ages of six and twelve. The patch is applied each morning, alternating hips with each application.

As effective as medications have proven to be, they are drugs and, as such, they have potential side effects.

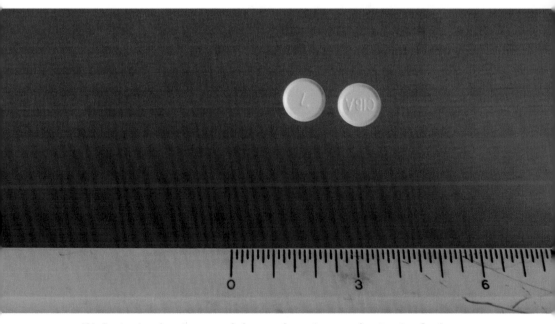

*If behavioral and environmental changes do not improve the situation for the child, medication is the next step in treatment. Ritalin is the most prescribed medication for treating ADHD.*

*Some people choose to try alternative therapies, such as an all-natural, additive-free diet, for the treatment of ADHD. However, there is no scientific proof that these treatments are effective.*

Liver disease, cardiac problems, and a rare but dangerous potential for suicide are some of the more serious side effects. Other potential side effects include insomnia, decreased appetite, stomachache, and irritability.

## Other Treatments

To maximize the effects of the medication, many doctors recommend other forms of therapy as well. These are usually considered as supplements rather than replacements for medications.

The most important non-medication treatment for children with ADHD usually occurs in the classroom. The school psychologist and a special education teacher will help create an individualized education plan (IEP) to meet the educational needs of each child with this disorder. The IEP will include activities for helping children like this monitor and control their own attention and behavior.

Other kinds of psychosocial treatments may be helpful as well. Psychotherapy, or counseling, helps children with ADHD to feel good about themselves and accept their disorder. Behavior modification techniques may help these children change their actual behaviors by giving praise or rewards every time they act in a desired way. Social skills training may also help these children learn new behaviors by practicing skills like sharing, taking turns, and learning to read others' facial expressions and tone of voice. Support groups can also help children with ADHD and their parents to feel better about their problems and understand that they are not alone. Parenting skills training gives parents tools for managing their children's behavior, like "time out," behavior modification techniques, and stress management techniques to help both their children and themselves handle their frustrations more effectively.

Because children with ADHD cannot self-regulate their emotions or behavior easily, the best support these children can be given involves structuring their environments, both at home and at school. Children with ADHD need reliable, consistent reinforcement for appropriate behavior. Reinforcement must be frequent and intense. (In other words, where the average child might be motivated to complete school tasks by the promise of a weekly sticker, children with ADHD tend to need larger and more frequent sources of motivation.) Long-term tasks need to be broken down into smaller, more manageable steps.

Alternative therapies for ADHD such as use of megavitamins, body treatments, special diets, *chiropractic* treatments, meditation, visual training, and psychotherapy have also been tried. To date, scientific research has not proven any of them to be effective therapeutic options. Ritalin continues to be the most common treatment for ADHD.

# 3 The Controversy Over ADHD

·HCl

During ADHD's early history, not everyone in the medical community agreed that the condition actually existed. Years of research have led most authorities to accept the condition as a medical fact.

That doesn't mean, however, that there is a **consensus** about ADHD. Although today most health-care professionals no longer doubt the condition exists, many experts disagree as to whether it is as **pervasive** as diagnoses might suggest. According to survey results released by the Centers for Disease Control and Prevention (CDC) in 2007, approximately 5.4 million children in the United States had ever been diagnosed with ADHD. Medical professionals who doubt the real prevalence of the disorder question whether ADHD has become a "catch-all" category for symptoms that cannot be categorized elsewhere and for which there may be other causes. Most of these arguments against ADHD's reality are also arguments against the use of Ritalin.

## Is Our Culture the Culprit?

Richard DeGrandpre wrote in his book *Ritalin Nation* that some of the symptoms of ADHD are actually ways individuals have devised to cope with the incredibly fast pace of the world today: "While the world has been speeding up, we as conscious, **temporal** beings have been speeding up with it . . . we cannot help internalizing and **emulating** the rhythm of our own surroundings." In other words, these behaviors are ways of keeping up with the rest of the world.

In neuropsychiatrist Sydney Walker's book *The Hyperactivity Hoax*, he refers to the rise of Ritalin as "symptoms of modern life, rather than symptoms of modern disease." DeGrandpre argues that Ritalin and ADHD are the inevitable by-products of our culture's addiction to speed, as indicated by everything from fast food to cellular phones, from faxes and overnight mail to faster-working computers, from rock music's fast beat to television shows that splice together images at hundredth-of-a-second intervals. Walker and DeGrandpre believe that as individuals are exposed to the rapid-fire pace of MTV, Nintendo®, and the rest of contemporary culture, they become **conditioned** to expect stimulus at a certain pace. School does not offer them the stimulus they need at the speed they need, and so they become bored.

Give ADHD kids something new and interesting to do, DeGrandpre argues, and they'll be fine. Walker recommends creating educational settings that mimic high-stimulus activities like television and video games, which, he writes, "constitute a strange sort of good-fit situation for distractible children. These activities are among the few things they can concentrate on well." Make their lives more interesting—and kids won't need Ritalin.

*Some researchers suspect that the increase in the numbers of individuals with ADHD is the result of our fast-paced world. With everything around us moving quicker, we need to find a way to speed up as well.*

Peter R. Breggin, a psychiatrist and founder of the International Center for the Study of Psychiatry and Psychology, claims that a child diagnosed as having ADHD actually has other problems. For example, if a student can't pay attention in class, perhaps she needs a teacher better equipped to hold her attention. These are kids being kids, Breggin believes, but school has changed to the point where it no longer meets children's needs. In a 2000 interview on PBS's *Frontline*, Breggin had this to say in reference to ADHD:

> We have lost track of what childhood is about, of what parenthood and teaching is about. We now think it's about having good quiet children who make it easy for us to go to work. It's about having submissive children who will sit in a boring classroom of 30, often with teachers who don't know how to use visual aids and all the other

## Huck Finn on Ritalin?

Dr. Larry Diller, author of *Running on Ritalin* asks, "Is there still a place for childhood in the anxious, downsizing America of the late nineteen-nineties? What if Tom Sawyer or Huckleberry Finn were to walk into my office tomorrow? Tom's indifference to schooling and Huck's 'oppositional' behavior would surely have been cause for concern. Would I prescribe Ritalin for them, too?"

Other experts, however, point out that Huck Finn and Tom Sawyer lived in an age where difficult children simply dropped out of school and went to work on farms—or drifted into lives of poverty and violence. Today, on the other hand, children are required to handle situations that demand attention and intellectual consideration, while at the same time, it is no longer considered appropriate simply to cast aside those who have difficulty coping. While the modern world increasingly values intellectual consideration and rationality, this tendency could be a good thing. According to this perspective, the modern world didn't create ADHD; it simply made obvious a problem that had always existed—and then sought to find a treatment for it.

exciting technologies that kids are used to. Or there are teachers who are forced to pressure their children to get grades on standardized tests, and don't have the time to pay individual attention to them. We're in a situation in America in which the personal growth and development and happiness of our children is not the priority; it's rather the smooth functioning of overstressed families and schools.

In Breggin's book *Talking Back to Ritalin*, he claims that there are no differences in the brains of children diagnosed with ADHD or in their chemical makeup. Where ADHD-like physical symptoms do occur, he states that they are caused by environmental factors such as lead poisoning or head injuries.

But many experts disagree—and they cite multiple research studies that support their views. When kids with ADHD are tested on activities like video games, for example, they don't actually demonstrate the "good fit" Sydney Walker predicted. When Rosemary Tannock, a behavioral scientist at the Hospital for Sick Children in Toronto, looked at how well a group of boys between the ages of eight and twelve actually did at video games, she found that the ones with ADHD completed fewer levels and had to restart more games than those without the disorder.

The cultural connection to ADHD is further disproved by the fact that research strongly indicates that this condition is genetically inherited. If modern culture were the reason for ADHD symptoms, it would make sense that children might have the condition while their parents did not—but this is not what studies have shown.

## ADHD as an Advantage

Other groups acknowledge that ADHD is a real biological condition—but they believe it should not necessarily be considered in a negative light. CHADD (Children and Adults with Attention Deficit/Hyperactivity Disorder) stresses that all people with ADHD have many talents and abilities that they can use to enhance their lives:

> many people with ADHD even feel that their patterns of behavior give them unique, often unrecognized, advantages. People with ADHD tend to be outgoing and ready for action. Because of their drive for excitement and stimulation, many become successful in business, sports, construction, and public speaking. Because of their ability to

*Some researchers argue that ADHD children would do fine in school if the environment mimicked the stimulating, fast-paced environment of video games. However, other studies have shown that ADHD children do not perform better on video games than their non-ADHD peers.*

think about many things at once, many have won acclaim as artists and inventors.

People who lean toward this view of ADHD often believe that history's great hunters, explorers, inventors, and politicians may have all experienced ADHD, that in fact, the qualities of ADHD were responsible for fueling these famous leaders' success. Dr. Edward Hallowell, who coauthored the book *Driven to Distraction: Recognizing and Coping with Attention Deficit Disorder from Childhood Through Adulthood*, agrees with this point of view. Hallowell has this to say about the hidden benefits of ADHD:

> ADD people are highly imaginative and intuitive. They have a "feel" for things, a way of seeing right to the heart of matters while others have to reason their way along methodically. . . . This is the man or woman who makes million-dollar deals in catnip and pulls them off the next day. This is the child who, having been reprimanded for blurting something out, is then praised for having blurted out something brilliant. . . . It is important for others to be sensitive to this "sixth sense" many ADD people have and to nurture it. If the environment insists on rational, linear thinking and "good" behavior from these kids all the time they may never develop their intuitive style to the point where they can use it profitably.

From this perspective, ADHD is considered an adaptive behavior. Unlike DeGrandpre and Walker, however, who see ADHD as an adaptation to *modern* culture, this perspective views ADHD as a collection of behaviors that evolved to meet survival needs in the past, behaviors which no longer fit well with today's culture and social expectations. Again, however, although the reasoning may be different, the end conclusion is the same: Ritalin is at best unnecessary and at worst downright evil.

But research does not support this view of ADHD either. According to Dr. Russell Barclay, in the thousands of peer-reviewed scientific studies dealing with ADHD over the past thirty years, not one found that individuals with ADHD performed better (as indicated by a valuable trait, asset, or behavior) than those without ADHD. People with ADHD can learn to live with their condition, and they can rise above it—but few experts believe that it should be seen as a blessing.

## ADHD and Health Insurance

Still other critics of ADHD indicate that such diagnoses may have another connection. The CDC report noted that ADHD was diagnosed less often in minority populations and among those who did not have health insurance. This leads some to believe that ADHD diagnoses are merely a way for the health industry to rake in money. When more cases of ADHD are diagnosed, the drug company that produces Ritalin is one of the most obvious financial beneficiaries.

There is some truth to the fact that once a condition has been diagnosed and medications are marketed to treat that condition, the condition becomes more easily recognized. For example, before the advent of antidepressant medications, people were diagnosed less often as suffering from depression. But complicated and intertwined factors are always at work with medical conditions like this. For instance, does ADHD actually occur less often in populations that lack health insurance—or are the lower number of diagnoses based on the fact that these populations may not have access to the testing procedures required to make the diagnosis? This is a question that requires additional research.

## ADHD and Medication

Perhaps the biggest area of controversy surrounds the treatment of ADHD. Though medication, especially Ritalin, is the most used treatment method, some in the health-care community question whether that is the right thing for the patient. Ritalin and the other medications prescribed for ADHD are not without risk, and some deaths have been attributed to them. Some health-care professionals and parents are searching for alternative treatments. One of the prominent ones centers on a special diet. Though claims that it can cure the condition cannot be proven, many individuals are convinced that their symptoms are alleviated by watching what they eat.

If people believe that ADHD stems from complicated cultural trends or societal factors, then it doesn't make sense that it could be cured with a pill. But if ADHD is actually caused by a particular physical problem in the brain, then perhaps chemical intervention is the right route after all.

Are ADHD medications overused? Or are they underused? Strangely enough, the answer to both questions is, "Yes." Some children are undoubtedly taking medication when their issues could be just as effectively addressed by behavioral interventions. At the same time, however, other children, whose lives could be made much easier with the help of medication, are needlessly facing the steep uphill battle that ADHD poses.

Children, teens, and adults with ADHD can find real relief from their symptoms through Ritalin. However, there is another group that uses Ritalin to find "relief"— the Ritalin abusers. Their reality only adds fuel to the Ritalin controversy.

# 4 Ritalin Abuse

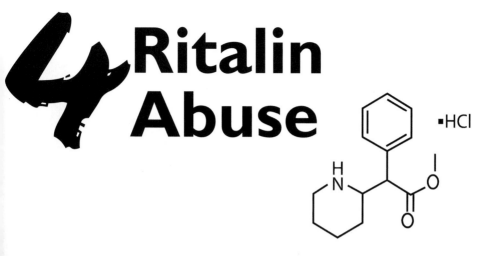

•HCl

At 10 p.m. on a Thursday night, Devon Burke sits at a desk in his apartment and pours over a study guide for a mathematical achievement test for prospective business school applicants. Though he is sleep-deprived from a week of working over 65 hours at his job at a bank, he feels alert and attentive. His focus is mainly thanks to Ritalin, a stimulant mostly prescribed to children with attention deficit hyperactivity disorder, or ADHD. But Burke does not have a prescription for Ritalin and he does not have ADHD.

"On Ritalin, your concentration is finely tuned and you can rebound after a big night out," said Burke, who gets his Ritalin from his sister. "But most people I know don't use it when they're drinking. In fact, it probably isn't good for you. People just want to get a leg up.

"People keep it close to the vest. . . . There's a stigma—real or perceived—that there is something wrong with using Ritalin."
(*Source:* Ted Weihman, "Ritalin Abuse Graduates from College," Columbia News Service, October 14, 2003)

Devon Burke is just one of the people who use Ritalin for nonmedical purposes. (The National Survey on Drug Use and Health (NSDUH) defines nonmedical use as occurring when an individual takes prescription medications that were not prescribed for her, or takes the medication only for the feeling—the "high"—that results from taking it.)

And Burke is not alone. According to the 2009 Monitoring the Future Survey (MTF), conducted among U.S. students, 1.8 percent of students in eighth grade have

## Abuse—or Misuse?

Abuse and misuse are two different things; unfortunately, both can lead to addiction.

### Misuse:
Patients may forget or not understand their prescription's directions. They may start making their own decisions, perhaps upping the dose in hopes of getting better faster.

### Abuse:
People may use prescription drugs for nonmedical reasons. Prescription drug abusers may obtain such drugs illegally and use them to get high, fight stress, or boost energy.

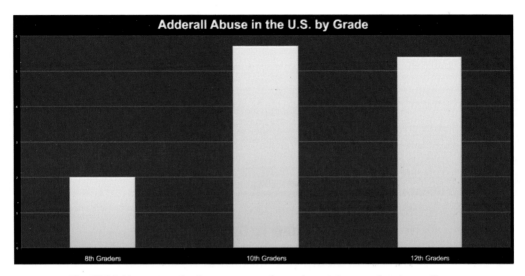

**Adderall Abuse in the U.S. by Grade**

| | | |
|---|---|---|
| 8th Graders | 10th Graders | 12th Graders |

*The 2009 Monitoring the Future survey also gathered data on the abuse of Adderall, another stimulant used to treat ADHD.*

abused Ritalin in the past year; 3.6 percent of those in tenth grade and 2.1 of twelfth-graders have as well. These figures show a slight decrease from the previous year of annual abuse of Ritalin by those in grades eight and twelve; statistics show an increase in use among tenth graders. Studies have indicated that nonmedical use of Ritalin occurs most often in boys, though between 2004 and 2005, use among girls increased. In Canada, 0.2% percent of the population had abused Ritalin in 2010. The percentage of high schoolers who had abused Ritalin was higher.

Although use seems to have leveled off somewhat in American teenagers, researchers are studying why the abuse of Ritalin has affected such a large number of young people.

## The Monitoring the Future Survey

Since 1975, the Monitoring the Future (MTF) Survey has measured drug, alcohol, and cigarette use and related attitudes among adolescent students nationwide. Survey participants report their drug use behaviors across three time periods: lifetime, past year, and past month. In 2009, over 46,000 students in grades 8, 10, and 12 from almost 400 secondary schools participated in the survey. The survey is funded by the National Institute on Drug Abuse, a component of the National Institutes of Health, and conducted by the University of Michigan.

### When It Began

How did a drug meant to help children get a good education and have a better life become a favorite recreational drug of students and others not diagnosed with ADHD? The nonmedical use of prescription medications has become a big problem in North America in the past few years.

Nonmedical use of Ritalin is not a product of the new millennium. Doctors W. Alexander Morton and Gwendolyn G. Stockton write in their article "Methylphenidate Abuse and Psychiatric Side Effects," that the potential for abusing methylphenidate was discussed in the early 1960s when a patient was reported as taking 125 tablets of the drug *each day*. Other reports of oral abuse of methylphenidate occurred in 1971. Professional publications then began reporting other cases of intravenous abuse of methylphenidate, including a death, in 1986. In 1991, the first case of intranasal abuse was reported. In 1996, the DEA began sounding warning bells when it warned that if Ritalin "fell into the wrong hands," abuse could be rampant, especially among high school students, college students, and recent college graduates looking for an "edge."

## Why It Began

The simple fact of the matter is that people would not use Ritalin nonmedically if there were not a perceived benefit attached to taking the drug. Ritalin is a mild stimulant and gives the abuser a slight high, not unlike what might be found in highly caffeinated drinks. In someone diagnosed with ADHD, this medically induced "kick" stimulates a part of the brain that isn't working correctly; it calms him down. In the person who does not have ADHD, such as Devon Burke, the young man introduced at the beginning of the chapter, the medication "kickstarts" his ability to focus and concentrate—long after others with his schedule would have gone to bed.

## A Brief History of Methylphenidate Abuse

| | |
|---|---|
| 1960 | oral addiction potential questioned |
| 1963 | intravenous abuse in the United States |
| 1968 | withdrawn from the Swedish market |
| 1971 | first report of oral abuse |
| 1971 | DEA monitors amount produced in the United States |
| 1971 | methylphenidate is classified as a Schedule II drug |
| 1986 | intravenous abuse resulting in death |
| 1988 | abuse by family members is reported |
| 1991 | first report of intranasal abuse |
| 1995 | intranasal use resulting in deaths |
| 1995 | intranasal use by adolescents |
| 1998 | student survey: 16% abusing |
| 1999 | intranasal abuse resulting in death |

(*Source:* W. Alexander Morton and Gwendolyn G. Stockton, "Methylphenidate Abuse and Psychiatric Side Effects," 2000.)

The ability to stay ahead of others is a major reason cited by many as the reason they began abusing Ritalin. This is a highly competitive world, and to get ahead—the goal of many people—requires long hours and lots of hard work. In the mid-1990s, college students on the East Coast found that taking Ritalin helped them balance all-night study sessions, jobs, and classes, and allowed for some all-night partying as well. Their parents might have used multiple cups of coffee and other high-caffeine drinks to accomplish the same goals when they were in college, but this younger generation of college students found Ritalin more effective.

**Street Names for Ritalin**

kibbles and bits
pineapple
Skippy
Smarties
vitamin R
R ball
kiddie cocaine
smart drug
cramming drug

It wasn't just American colleges and universities that began to notice a problem with Ritalin abuse on their campuses. In 1998, McGill University, a highly prestigious and very competitive university in Montreal, Canada, was one of the first universities to report that some of their students were illegally using Ritalin. In a 2005 interview in *The Gateway*, Norman Hoffman, director of the university's mental health center, reported that its use continues, and

> he regularly sees students who claim to have problems concentrating, have heard and read about attention deficit hyperactivity disorder . . . and ask for a prescription. . . . But many students,

*Many students use Ritalin for the same reason that their parents drink coffee. It is a stimulant that helps keep them awake and focused enough to complete papers or study for exams.*

**Recreational Ritalin—The Not-So-Smart Drug 73**

*Students use Ritalin to gain an edge over their classmates in college. After college, the level of competition only increases, as young graduates battle with the entire workforce for jobs and recognition.*

seeking an edge in academic competition, bypass the route to a Ritalin prescription and simply obtain the drug illegally, often from friends. . . .

Hoffman is also concerned about the issue underlying Ritalin abuse—that students feel they need to use a stimulant in order to do well in school. Students who abuse Ritalin, according to Hoffman, are not satisfied with their natural abilities: they have a sense of inadequacy, a sense of pressure that is often carried throughout life.

One McGill student used Ritalin as a study aid for a particularly difficult exam during his first semester: "I remember feeling great. . . . It did the job." He also didn't see taking Ritalin as becoming a regular habit, saying that he had taken it because he was "desperate." He admitted, however, that he didn't plan on stopping any time soon: "When would I stop [using Ritalin]? . . . It's not like life suddenly gets easier after university."

Not all abuse of Ritalin in college is related to seemingly noble reasons such as doing well and getting a job. Recreational use of Ritalin on college campuses is also a problem. In a study conducted in 2006 at a northeastern university, more than 16 percent of the students surveyed admitted to abusing stimulant medications; 96 percent of these students preferred Ritalin. The study found that among **traditional college students**, Ritalin abuse rates appeared to be the same as those for cocaine and amphetamines.

After college students graduate and entere the job market, competition does not ease. If anything, it increases. After all, the only people against whom a young adult has to compete at the school are fellow students. Once someone enters the "real world," however, competition comes at him from the job market all over the country and, in some cases, even internationally. For some, taking Ritalin helps them work extra hours, hoping to get a leg up on the competition.

As in the case of college students, some new to the workforce also take Ritalin for recreational purposes. According to investment analyst Miguel Anderson, who is quoted on the website www.jrn.columbia.edu, "I have a few friends here and there that use it [Ritalin] for various purposes. . . . I know one person who uses it occasionally at work, perhaps after a late Thursday night as well as occasionally on weekends, but not for big rallies, just to get by when tired."

Eventually, nonmedical use of Ritalin expanded beyond the East Coast. It also expanded its user base to include high school students. Like the college student Ritalin abuser, high school students for whom Ritalin was the drug of choice also sought a high—a good feeling. But also like the college students, some abused the drug to get an edge on the college-bound competition. Entry into the best, most prestigious colleges can be very selective, and some high school students are willing to pay almost any price for it. This includes studying to get the highest grades possible; doing volunteer work and participating in sports or other extracurricular activities to beef up that part of the college application; and working to get some spending money to put toward a car or college expenses. Ritalin helps ambition-driven students accomplish all those things. Of course some high school students also abuse Ritalin recreationally, attracted only by its high.

But with a smorgasbord of other drugs available for recreational use, there has to be something about Ritalin that makes it attractive to the drug-taking public.

### Availability

According to the Johns Hopkins University November 22, 2002 newsletter, in 2002, more than seven million children in the United States took more than eight tons of Ritalin every year. Since then, the number of prescriptions written in the United States has increased dramatically. Although fewer prescriptions for Ritalin are written in Canada, approximately 950,000 in 2005, it is still one of the most-prescribed medications in that country as well. This adds up to one of the major reasons why Ritalin has become so abused—availability. With more perscriptions being written, there are more potential sources of the medication for people without prescriptions.

According to the DEA, most Ritalin intended for abuse comes from legitimately obtained supplies. Some-

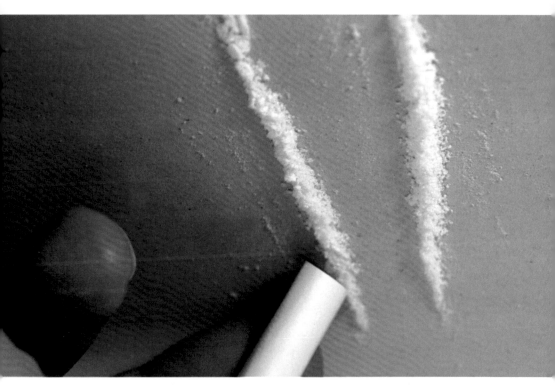

*While the pill form is the most commonly abused, Ritalin is also snorted or injected with a needle.*

one who wants to abuse the drug gets it from someone who takes the medication for ADHD or one of the other conditions for which it is prescribed. Siblings, even parents, in many households take the drug to treat ADHD. All someone wanting to abuse the drug would have to do is reach in the medicine cabinet and take pills out of the bottle. And it's not just non-ADHD siblings sneaking Ritalin from the medicine cabinets. In some cases, parents are taking the pills, having discovered the same qualities that make them attractive to teenage abusers.

A 2002 survey found that most Wisconsin schools did not control access to Ritalin brought to school by students for whom it was prescribed. Students had little difficulty giving away, stealing, or selling it.

Budding *entrepreneurs* may sell their pills from their own prescriptions for a few bucks. Middle school, high school, and college students can sell their prescription Ritalin to others for $1 to $5 or more for one pill. It's a way to make money, and it spreads Ritalin abuse around schools.

"Doctor shopping," the practice of going to different doctors to get prescriptions, is another way of getting Ritalin. Some enterprising individuals have simply told an unethical doctor that they think they *might* have ADHD and walked out with a prescription, thereby eliminating the middleman.

Theft is another way of obtaining Ritalin. According to the U.S. Department of Justice, nearly two thousand cases of Ritalin theft were reported between January 1990 and May 1995, putting it in the top-ten of most-stolen controlled substances.

Ritalin is approved by the FDA and prescribed by thousands of doctors every year. However, it is dangerous when taken incorrectly.

## How Ritalin Is Abused

Ritalin is usually taken in its easiest and simplest form—as a pill. However, people can inject the drug directly into their veins; they also can "snort" Ritalin.

The first case of intravenous abuse of methylphenidate was reported in 1963 (along with the psychosis that came with it). The pills or tablets were crushed into a powder, mixed with water, and then injected with a hypodermic needle.

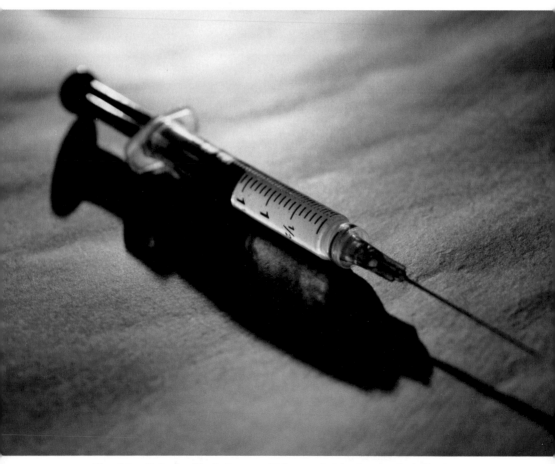

*The risks of abusing Ritalin increase if the user is injecting the drug. Sharing hypodermic needles puts the user at risk of contracting a disease such as HIV.*

Besides popping a pill, the easiest way to abuse Ritalin and other forms of methylphenidate is to crush the pills or tablets and inhale the powder. Reports of this type of abuse did not begin to appear in the professional literature until the early 1990s. In 1991, the first case of intranasal abuse of methylphenidate was reported: for two years, a sixteen-year-old boy had been using his prescribed Ritalin to get high. At the time the case was reported, he was up to a daily intranasal dose of 200 milligrams.

No matter how the drug is taken into the body, abuse means risk.

### Risks of Ritalin Abuse

It's prescribed to millions of children in the United States alone; it's prescribed by a health-care professional; it's approved by the FDA—part of the U.S. government. So how harmful can it be?

These comments are examples of the faulty logic many Ritalin abusers use when discussing the safety of their drug of choice. Yes, millions of children do take Ritalin; yes, it is prescribed by a health-care professional; yes, it has been approved by the FDA. But, that doesn't mean it will not cause harm when taken in ways other than as prescribed.

Drug abuse and the drug problem are not limited to selling and using drugs such as cocaine or heroin or even anabolic steroids. One of the biggest drug problems today is the abuse of prescription medications. The nonmedical use of prescription drugs has increased dramatically in the past few years. According to the NSDUH, in 2009 an estimated 4.3 million Americans used prescription drugs for nonmedical purposes for the first time.

The risks of abusing Ritalin and other methylphenidates come from how the drug is abused as well as the characteristics of the drugs themselves. The person who injects Ritalin runs the risk of contracting HIV if she shares needles. More common are complications caused by the pills' fillers, which do not dissolve in water. When the solution is injected, these particles can block tiny blood vessels, causing damage to the lungs and even to the eyes. If the powder is inhaled, nasal passages can become irritated. In some cases, lung damage has been reported.

Many people who abuse Ritalin and other prescription medications are lulled into a false sense of security simply by the fact that these drugs require a prescription by a physician or other health-care professional. However, that does not make them safe. When a child or adult is prescribed Ritalin, the health-care provider has done a workup on the individual, taking into account other issues such as her overall general health and degree of disability, for example. Once the health-care provider has this information, she can prescribe the dosage that will work best to treat the person's condition.

What might be a safe prescription for someone with a specific condition might not be so safe for someone without that condition. Remember how Ritalin works in the brain of someone diagnosed with ADHD: it calms the

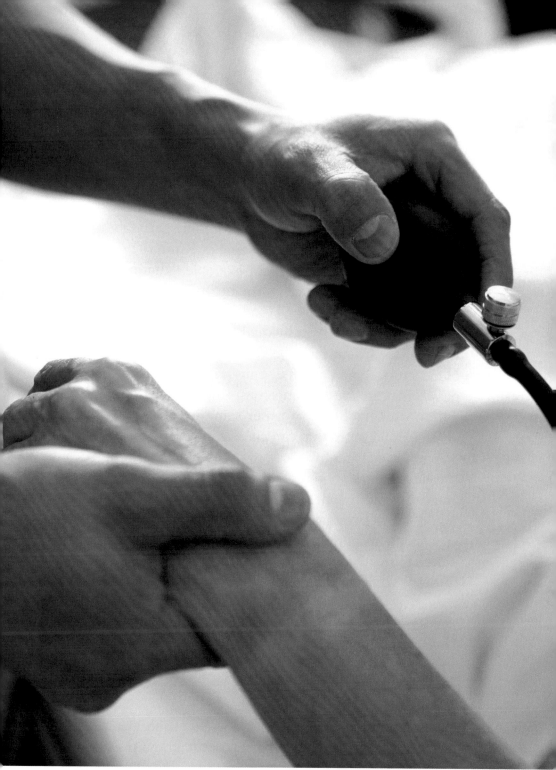

*There are many potentially dangerous side effects of taking Ritalin. The drug can cause the heart to beat rapidly and irregularly and may increase blood pressure enough to cause a stroke.*

**Recreational Ritalin—The Not-So-Smart Drug 83**

individual, stemming hyperactivity and other character-istics of the disorder. But in someone without ADHD, someone in whom the dopamine levels are not compro-mised, attention levels may increase, he may feel more energetic, more "raring to go"—all the things that make taking Ritalin attractive to overworked and frustrated students (as well as those looking for more party-ability). But while doing those things, some of Ritalin's other ef-fects can be less attractive. For example, Ritalin can af-fect blood pressure and cause the heart to beat irregularly or too fast. In some cases, blood pressure can increase so dramatically that the individual may suffer a *stroke*. Al-though rare, there have been reports of cases in which blood pressure actually fell, causing a loss of conscious-ness. This can also be dangerous, since the person might fall and hit his head, or suffer some other accident. A change in heart rhythm can cause a heart attack, even in a child or teenager.

Although the potential physical side effects of Ritalin and other methylphenidates are fairly well known, that is not true of psychiatric reactions to their abuse. Psychi-atric side effects that have been reported resemble ones associated with amphetamine and cocaine abuse. Some of the psychiatric side effects of methylphenidate abuse include:

- extreme anger with threats of violence
- delirium
- panic attacks

Many of Ritalin's potential side effects are described in chapter 1. Health-care professionals know that they should be on the lookout for those in the patients for whom they prescribe the medication. They also know that they must make certain their patients and the patients' families are aware that these side effects may appear. With such information, everyone can be prepared. But, when someone is abusing the drug, and there is no health-care supervision, it is impossible to prepare for the ill-effects that might occur.

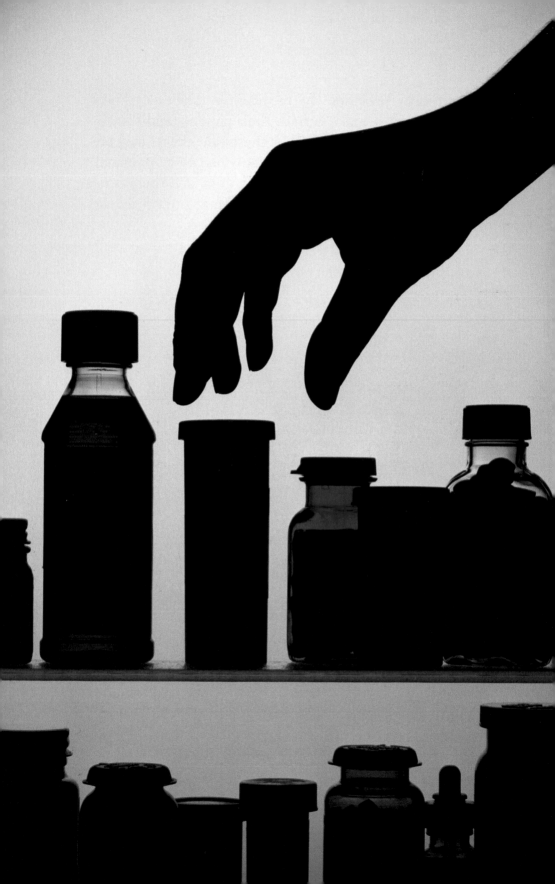

# 5 Treatment and Prevention

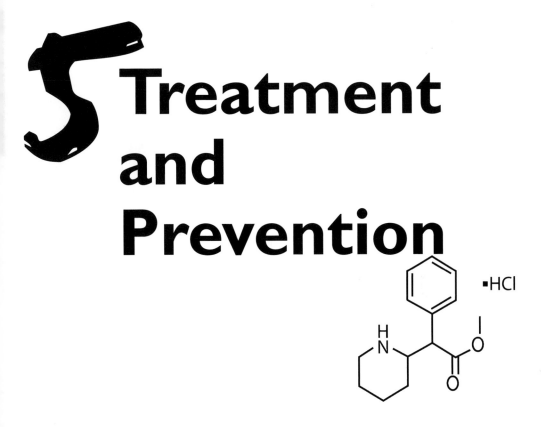

•HCl

For someone whose life centers around getting, taking, and getting more of a drug, there is little time left for actually living, taking advantage of good opportunities as they arise. When life reaches this stage, it's time for treatment.

## Tolerance, Dependency, and Addiction

The **vernacular** surrounding drugs and drug abuse can be confusing. When discussing drug abuse, the words tolerance, dependency, and addiction are often bandied about in such a way they may seem to mean the same thing. They most definitely do not.

After taking some medications for a period of time, a person may build up a tolerance to the drug. This means that her body needs to have more of the drug to achieve the same effect. Should tolerance develop when Ritalin is taken as prescribed, a health-care provider will adjust the dosage or perhaps prescribe a different drug.

If someone stops taking a drug and experiences withdrawal symptoms, her body has developed a dependency on that drug. Again, her health-care provider can help. By following the instructions of the health-care professional, dependence can be easily treated and withdrawal symptoms minimized and possibly eliminated with proper dosage adjustments.

Sometimes the need for the drug is more than physical. If an individual must take the drug in order to satisfy emotional *and* psychological needs, he has become addicted to the substance. An individual addicted to a drug has a **compulsive** need to use that specific medication for nonmedical purposes; the drug is taken because of its mood-altering effects—how he feels after he has taken the drug—not to relieve the symptoms of diagnosed ADHD. If Ritalin isn't available, he'll feel cravings and panic. His behavior can become erratic, and he may begin to lie, steal prescription pads, forge doctors' signatures, and doctor shop. He may return to his health-care provider and tell her he "lost" his medication, that it fell into the toilet, or

**Ritalin withdrawal symptoms can include:**

- agitation
- sleeplessness
- abdominal cramps
- nausea
- depression
- exhaustion
- anxiety

*Dependence is the physical need for a drug, while addiction is the psychological or emotional need. Often an individual who is addicted will feel depressed in between her doses of the drug.*

even that his dog ate it—all with the goal of getting more of the drug.

Ritalin dependence and addiction can be characterized by the need for increasingly higher doses of the drug and increasingly frequent **binges**. Between binges, those abusing the drug often fall into deep depressions. The only way out of that depression is more Ritalin—or treatment.

The first step in overcoming addiction to any substance—drugs, alcohol, tobacco, food, even sex—is to admit there is a problem, that one is an addict. For many, this is the hardest in a series of incredibly hard steps. But it is impossible to find sobriety, to live a life Ritalin free, without first admitting to being an addict. Many people with addictions complete programs without using the word "addict" to describe themselves, and experts say staying clean for those people may be a long shot.

## Detoxification

Once an individual has decided to break free from addiction, the body must go through a process of withdrawal to rid itself of the toxic substances of the drug. Through a medically supervised process called detoxification, the individual goes through some or all of the withdrawal symptoms listed earlier in this book. How long withdrawal lasts depends on how much and how often Ritalin was taken.

For someone who is dependent on Ritalin, this process might be enough to prevent further misuse. Someone who is addicted to Ritalin, however, needs follow-up treatment; studies have shown that most people with addictions will return to their previous behaviors if treatment ends with detoxification. For many addictions, there are two primary methods of treating addiction: behavioral and pharmacological. There is no proven *pharmacological* treatment for Ritalin abuse, however. For those addicted to Ritalin, rehabilitation comes in the form of behavioral therapy.

**Fast Facts**

Dependency is physical.
Addiction is psychological.
Being dependent on a drug does not mean you'll always become addicted to the substance.

## Behavioral Treatment Programs

Put simply, behavioral treatment programs teach people with addictions how to change their behaviors so they are less likely to repeat the ones that led to addiction. Unfortunately, nothing about any type of addiction is simple. There are many kinds of behavioral treatment programs, but several themes are common: commitment to drug abstinence; learning to avoid people, places, and situations that are associated with drug use; finding substitute behaviors to fill the "void" left by the drugs; and building new supportive social networks. Some programs emphasize religion, others stress occupational skill building, and still others may focus on behavioral self-control techniques. Some rely heavily on a type of counseling termed "motivational interviewing" pioneered by Dr. James Miller. Some rely on helping people make progress through what are termed "stages of change" in the addiction from drug use to a new life, as pioneered by Drs. Carlo DiClemente and James Prochaska. **Cognitive**-behavioral therapy helps the individuals recognize how thought patterns influence behaviors. Behavioral contingency programs find ways to help motivate and sustain drug abstinence.

Although there are strong advocates of each of these programs and more, the important thing to recognize is that different people respond better to different programs and that if one does not seem to fit, then rather than giving up or blaming the failure on the drug user, another program should be found. Though behavioral treatment programs do help those with addictions find ways to avoid behaviors that can cause a **relapse**, they also need to help them discover what led to those behaviors initially. With therapy, individuals learn how to change

Addiction treatment programs often begin with a stay in an inpatient treatment center. While there, the patient is secluded from the outside world so he can learn about himself and his addiction.

negative thought patterns, thereby changing behaviors. Individual and family therapy can help the person with addiction and those around her. Therapy can also help the addicted individual and her friends and family handle relapses, since most people do relapse at some point during recovery.

It is very important for people with addictions to Ritalin to acknowledge truthfully why they take the drug. Were they among those looking for a "party high"? Or were they looking for a way to get an edge on the competition—to study or work longer hours? Only if they are honest with themselves can individuals learn to avoid the enabling behaviors and adopt those that will help them live a life free of Ritalin.

Behavioral treatment programs often begin with a period of inpatient treatment. Depending on the length, severity, and drug of addiction, inpatient treatment can be short-term (usually a minimum of thirty days) or long-term residential. At first, some programs allow inpatients to have minimal—if any—contact with the "outside world." Patients concentrate on learning about themselves and their relationship with the drug. Later, family and perhaps close friends are encouraged to participate in the treatment program.

Beginning even during inpatient treatment, people with addictions are encouraged to supplement their programs with support groups such as Narcotics Anonymous.

## Narcotics Anonymous

Based on the twelve-step program of Alcoholics Anonymous (AA), Narcotics Anonymous (NA) helps those addicted to drugs, including Ritalin, stay sober in the outside world. The first NA meetings were held in the early 1950s in Los Angeles, California. As found on its website (www.na.org), the organization described itself this way in its first publication:

> NA is a nonprofit fellowship or society of men and women for whom drugs had become a major problem. We . . . meet regularly to help each other stay clean. . . . We are not interested in what or how much you used . . . but only in what you want to do about your problem and how we can help.

In the more than half a century since it was founded, NA has grown into one of the largest organizations of its kind. Today, groups are located all over the world, and its books and pamphlets are published in thirty-two languages. No matter where the group is located, each chapter is based on the twelve steps first formulated in AA:

1. We admitted we were powerless over drugs—that our lives had become unmanageable.
2. Came to believe that a Power greater than ourselves could restore us to sanity.
3. Made a decision to turn our will and our lives over to the care of God as we understand Him.
4. Made a searching and fearless moral inventory of ourselves.
5. Admitted to God, and to ourselves, and to another human being the exact nature of our wrongs.
6. We're entirely ready to have God remove all these defects of character.
7. Humbly asked Him to remove our shortcomings.
8. Made a list of all persons we had harmed, and became willing to make amends to them all.

*After the initial seclusion, family and close friends are allowed to take part in the individual's recovery. Also, the individual is encouraged to attend a support group, such as Narcotics Anonymous.*

9. Made direct amends to such people wherever possible, except when to do so would injure them or others.
10. Continued to take personal inventory and when we were wrong promptly admitted it.
11. Sought through prayer and meditation to improve our conscious contact with God as we understand Him, praying only for knowledge of His will for us and the power to carry that out.
12. Having had a spiritual awakening as the result of these steps, we tried to carry this message to other drug addicts and to practice these principles in all our affairs.

Though participation in NA meetings will not guarantee a recovery free from temptation and relapse, these meetings can play an important role in staying sober. Should there not be an NA group in the area, recovering addicts are encouraged to attend AA meetings. Teenage children of those with Ritalin addictions are welcome at Alateen meetings. Other family members can find help through Al-Anon.

Although effective treatment methods such as NA are available, the best way to deal with Ritalin addiction is to avoid it in the first place.

## Prevention

When a drug is as prevalent in society as Ritalin is, almost inevitably, some will choose to abuse it. Look at other drugs in our culture: tobacco went from being a spiritual substance sacred to Native Americans to one of the world's most dangerous and addictive substances; alcohol can be used culturally without any danger—and yet it too can be addictive and destructive when abused. Prescription cough medicines are abused, as are painkillers. Potentially beneficial chemical substances can play positive roles in our culture—but they can play extremely negative roles as well. It all depends on how human beings make use of them.

Probably the most powerful way to prevent the misuse and abuse of ADHD medications is for the parents and guardians of youths who are prescribed these drugs to become more actively involved in monitoring their children's use. Too often, caregivers leave medicine use up to their children; the adults lose track of where the pills are and how fast they are being used. At the same time, youth can play an important role by helping their

*Controlling the abuse of Ritalin in schools is a challenging task. School nurses are supposed to distribute pills to students with prescriptions, but these pills can be stolen, or students can sell their pills outside of school.*

caregivers set up monitoring systems that are practical for their situations. These systems can help make sure that medicines such as Ritalin are properly used and accounted for—and that they are not being diverted for misuse (either by their children or by others).

The DEA has put in place restrictions on how often a Ritalin prescription can be filled, and how many pills can be dispensed with each prescription. In most schools, students must turn in their Ritalin to the school nurse, who then dispenses it according to instructions from the parents (generally according to the orders of the prescribing physician). Unfortunately, this process has not always run smoothly; after all, schools were not intended to be pharmacies. Pills are sometimes stolen from teachers' desks and nurses' offices. Students prescribed Ritalin may sell some of their pills on the way to school.

In an attempt to provide guidelines to schools on how to handle this new responsibility (or burden, depending on one's perspective), the DEA compiled a list of recommendations:

- Schools should consider prohibiting students from carrying ADHD medication to or from the school. This would necessitate having a parent, guardian, or other responsible adult transport these medications to and from the school.
- ADHD medication should be provided to the school in a properly labeled container that identifies the name of the medication, the dosage to be administered and the frequency of administration.
- One person (preferably the school nurse) should maintain primary control of the medication supply. An incoming/outgoing medication inventory log would enable school staff to track amounts of medications

received and dispensed. A log could be maintained that indicates:

1. the name and strength of the medication received by the clinic;
2. the amount of medication received by or removed from the school (a physical count of the medication would be conducted in the presence of the parent or guardian. This same adult would initial and date the medication log);
3. the dates of dispensing; and
4. the name of the student to whom it was dispensed.

- Schools should consider not permitting a student to self-administer ADHD medication outside the presence of school staff so that verification can be made that the medication has, in fact, been consumed.
- The drug supply should be secured by means such as a locked room, drawer or cabinet. Non-duplicative keys to the locked drug storage area should be limited, and an inventory and accountability system for these keys should be maintained.
- Unused medication not removed from the school by a parent or other responsible adult should be destroyed by the school nurse. It is advisable that the destruction of the medication be witnessed by at least one other person and documented.

These are good suggestions—but with many schools understaffed, schools have not always been able to implement all the DEA's recommendations.

In an attempt to stem the tide of Ritalin abuse, the U.S. Department of Education's Higher Education Center for Alcohol and Other Drug Prevention devised a list of strategies for reducing abuse by giving secondary

*Educating students about the dangers of misusing Ritalin is one of the most important steps in preventing its abuse.*

## 100 Chapter 5—Treatment and Prevention

and college students options for relaxing, having fun, and getting involved:

1. Promote alcohol- and other drug-free social, recreational, and extracurricular options and public service.

   - Sponsor alcohol- and other drug-free social and recreational options for students. Marketing efforts for these events must clearly specify the alcohol- and other drug-free guidelines for the activities.
   - Sponsor and publicize volunteer and community service opportunities for students.

2. Create a social, academic, and residential environment that promotes healthy social norms.

   - Survey students to determine the prevalence of Ritalin and other prescription drug abuse on campus.
   - Offer resources to educate students about the dangers of Ritalin abuse.
   - Develop social norms marketing campaigns to address any exaggerated misperceptions of Ritalin and other prescription drug abuse.

3. Limit availability and access.

   - Work with local law enforcement to stay informed about trends relating to Ritalin abuse and theft in the area.
   - Work with campus health officials and doctors to monitor students' Ritalin requests.

*Many students cite stress over schoolwork as the reason that they turn to Ritalin. As a result, some colleges are offering workshops to teach students healthy ways to handle stress and anxiety.*

**102 Chapter 5—Treatment and Prevention**

4. Enforce campus policy and state and local laws.

- Revise campus alcohol and other drug policies as necessary to include commonly abused prescription drugs specifically.
- Communicate campus alcohol and other drug policies clearly and frequently to the community, including possible consequences for violations.

Many colleges are taking a **proactive** approach to drug abuse and other potential health problems by conducting workshops on how to handle stress, anxiety, tension—some of the very reasons individuals give for taking Ritalin. And for those who use Ritalin in order to have the energy to do extra projects, many colleges offer workshops or classes on how to better organize and schedule time.

Some might say that the most effective way to rid the world of Ritalin abuse would be to rid the world of Ritalin. We've already examined the controversies that surround ADHD, the condition for which Ritalin is most prescribed, and many of these controversies cling to the drug as well. Ritalin, however, also has its own set of controversies.

# 6 The Controversies

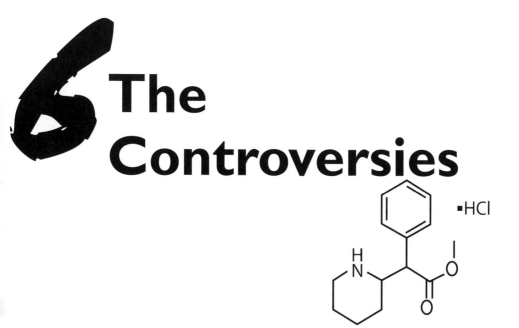

•HCl

Even if ADHD is a real condition (which some parents and authors are unwilling to accept), not everyone agrees that it should be treated with Ritalin. Critics believe that the reason ADHD is diagnosed so often is because people are looking for Ritalin prescriptions.

## Overdiagnosis and Overprescription

A large and vocal minority of Americans believe that Ritalin is overprescribed. There is no doubt that the number of Ritalin prescriptions written in the last few years has grown enormously in North America. Some, such as Joan Wolforth, director of the Centre for Students with Disabilities at McGill University in Toronto, claim there may be a rush to diagnose. According to Wolforth, "What may be happening is that because it's very much on the public eye, some people may be jumping to make a diagnosis [of ADHD]."

In his interview on *Frontline*, author Peter Breggin gave his opinion of drugs such as Ritalin:

> There are no miracle drugs. Speed—these drugs are forms of speed—don't improve human life. They reduce human life. And if you want less of a child, these drugs are very effective. These parents have also been lied to: flat-out lied to. They've been told that children have a neurobiological disorder. They've been told their children have biochemical imbalances and genetic defects. On what basis? That they fit into a checklist of attention deficit disorder, which is just a list of behaviors that teachers would like to see stopped in a classroom? That's all it is.

It's not just controversial authors who are expressing skepticism at the numbers of ADHD diagnoses and of prescriptions written for Ritalin. Superstars are joining in the chorus. Although they may have little if any special knowledge of these drugs, their views can have great impact because of their stardom and media coverage. These stars include:

- the late grunge-rocker Kurt Cobain, who was prescribed Ritalin beginning at age seven. Cobain believed that the drug led to his later abuse of related substances.
- Courtney Love, Cobain's widow and a rocker in her own right, was prescribed Ritalin as a child: "When you're a kid and you get this drug that makes you feel

that [euphoric] feeling, where else are you going to turn when you're an adult?"

- Marshall Mathers, bad-boy rapper Eminem, allegedly told radio talk-show host Howard Stern that his mother "misdiagnosed him with attention deficit disorder. My mother said I was a hyper kid, and I wasn't. She put me on Ritalin." One Eminem hit called "Cleaning Out My Closet" includes the lyric, "My whole life I was made to believe I was sick when I wasn't."

Many people believe an ADHD diagnosis is just an attempt to control unwanted behaviors. These skeptics argue that these children do not have a neurological disorder, but are just kids who don't conform to the expectations of parents and teachers.

*Some people believe that a Ritalin prescription in childhood will lead to the abuse of other substances. However, many studies indicate that the opposite is true.*

## Myths About Kids with ADHD and Psychostimulant Medications

**Myth:** Can lead to drug addiction later in life.
**Fact:** Since these drugs help many children succeed better at school, home, and play, avoiding negative experiences may actually help prevent future addictions to harmful drugs.

**Myth:** Responding well to this medication means a person has ADHD.
**Fact:** These medications allow many people to focus better, whether or not they have ADHD, but the improvement is more noticeable in people with ADHD.

**Myth:** Medication should be stopped when a child reaches adolescence.
**Fact:** About 80 percent of those who needed medication as children still need it as teenagers, and 50 percent will need it as adults.

**Myth:** Medication will make children "foggy" and dull-acting.
**Fact:** Children with ADHD who take these medications usually seem more alert, since they are better able to focus and pay attention.

**Myth:** These drugs have frequent dangerous side effects even when used properly.
**Fact:** Research indicates that these drugs are usually safe when used as directed under a doctor's supervision. They are quickly excreted by the body, and what side effects they may have are mild and do not threaten a child's well-being.

(Adapted from the National Institute of Mental Health's "Attention Deficit Hyperactivity Disorder." NIH Publication No. 96-3572, 2006.)

Perhaps the largest group voicing objection to the use of Ritalin is the Church of Scientology. Famous Scientologists such as actors Tom Cruise, Kelly Preston, and Priscilla Presley have been outspoken opponents to the use of Ritalin. Cruise, in an infamous interview on NBC's *Today Show*, referred to psychiatry as a **pseudoscience** and condemned the use of prescription drugs for psychiatric conditions.

Undoubtedly, some truth lies in the concern that people are sometimes given prescriptions for these drugs without proper diagnoses or an initial attempt to address the problem with behavioral interventions alone. However, charges like these do a terrible disservice to the many millions of young people with ADHD whose lives and potential to succeed and contribute to society can be greatly enhanced by the proper use of such medicines. People who claim that ADHD medication should never be used make about as much sense as if they insisted that a person dying of a bacterial infection should not be given an antibiotic because antibiotics are sometimes over-prescribed.

The U.S. Congress has stepped into the Ritalin prescription controversy. Parents who felt their children's schools were telling them they had to either put their child on Ritalin or a Ritalin-like drug or keep them out of school petitioned Congress to pass a law prohibiting such a *"Hobson's choice."* On December 4, 2004, President George W. Bush signed the "Prohibition on Mandatory Medication Amendment," which then became part of the IDEA. The amendment requires states and local educational authorities to implement policies that prohibit public schools from making a child's school attendance contingent on taking Ritalin or any other controlled substance.

Adolescents diagnosed with ADHD who are not treated have higher rates of speeding tickets and car accidents. Ritalin may be controversial, but research indicates that it is beneficial to many individuals.

*Ritalin continues to spark controversy. If you have to make a decision about Ritalin, make sure you are well informed; consult the Internet, read articles and talk to your doctor.*

## The School Experience

In *The LCP Solution The Remarkable Nutritional Treatment for ADHD, Dyslexia and Dyspraxia*, B. Jacqueline Stordy and Malcolm J. Nicholl cite a study done by Russell Barkley, concluding that 46 percent of untreated ADHD patients have been suspended and 11 percent have been expelled. No wonder, they say, that for children with ADHD, "school too often starts with failure ... and goes downhill from there."

According to some of those concerned with the increasing numbers of Ritalin prescriptions, one important consequence is that research on other potential treatments for ADHD is being neglected. Alternative treatments include nutritional and massage therapies. Though their efficacy has not been proven, their proponents believe they are viable treatment options to those seeking a nonpharmaceutical method of treating ADHD.

### Dangerous Side Effects

According to the website What Drugmakers Don't Want You to Know (www.ritalindeath.com/ADHD-Drug-Deaths.htm), thousands of children have died from using drugs used to treat ADHD, including Ritalin. According to statistics on that site, 186 children died between 1990 and 2000 as a result of taking those drugs. Also included on the site, which was created in memory of those who died from drugs used to treat ADHD, are guidelines for parents who feel their child died from ADHD-related medications, including how to pick a jury.

Most experts, however, would say that the statistics on the website are false or misinterpreted. Yes, they would agree, Ritalin has side effects, some of them very serious—but so do many other beneficial drugs. The FDA recently produced a study that set the risk of sudden death from Ritalin at 1 in 10,000 children. Potentially dangerous side effects can be minimized with proper monitoring by health-care professionals—and the benefits to an individual's life can be enormous.

## Ritalin and Other Addictions

Some people believe that if a child begins taking a medication while young, it sets him up to abuse other drugs, including tobacco and alcohol. This has not been proven when it comes to taking Ritalin. Most experts think the opposite is the case. When taking Ritalin or another methylphenidate allows the child to pay attention in class, do her homework, and participate in extracurricular activities, the child's self-esteem grows. Low self-esteem is one factor in determining who will abuse drugs.

Although ADHD and Ritalin are both the subject of controversy, it's hard to argue with success. Most scientific researchers today agree that medications such as Ritalin are the best treatment options for children and adolescents with ADHD. Studies indicate that many children with ADHD who have not been treated will eventually have higher rates of:

- substance abuse
- academic and professional failure
- relationship problems
- legal problems

The abuse of Ritalin, as any drug, is a serious concern. However, when used correctly, Ritalin helps thousands of individuals to lead happier, more productive lives.

**Recreational Ritalin—The Not-So-Smart Drug** 115

Research also indicates that treating ADHD with stimulants actually decreases the risk of alcohol and substance use disorders—while adolescents diagnosed with ADHD who are left untreated have much higher rates of:

• car accidents
• school failure
• speeding tickets

A large study that compared treatment methods for ADHD found that medication alone and medication plus intensive behavioral therapy proved to be equal in effectiveness—and both were superior to behavioral treatment alone and community-based treatment.

Other studies indicate the toll taken on families where a child with ADHD is left untreated:

• parents often have to reduce their work hours
• parents may be forced to change jobs or stop working all together
• parents experience high levels of marital discord

Thanks to Ritalin, many students are getting a good education and making friends, while adults are living productive lives.

Ellen Kingsley, an Emmy Award–winning journalist who retired when her son was diagnosed with ADHD, is one of the more outspoken proponents for the use of Ritalin. When her son's ADHD was first diagnosed, she was strongly against using medications. Now, however, she credits medication with making her son happy and well-adjusted. Kingsley likens the current debate over ADHD to the one over depression in an earlier decade. "We know now . . . [ADHD is] a neurobiological disorder that is correctable, not curable," she writes, and asserts that people with ADHD do not just have trouble paying attention in class. Instead, their "thinking isn't organized, working memory is affected." In a press conference for the National Consumers' League, Kingsley described her personal experiences:

> I read what appeared to be scientific information that AD/HD didn't exist, that it was a made-up disorder designed to make money for drug companies and doctors. I read, too, that the medicines were dangerous and that I ran the risk of turning my child into a zombie or an addict should I decide to let him try them. Besides, who wants to give a five-year-old a psychoactive medication?
>
> It took a lot of convincing, a lot of education and a lot of reading and then many months of watching my child suffer, unable to learn, unable to socialize normally, but able to make himself understood before I finally decided that it was worth it to give it a shot. . . . Today I'm happy to report that T.K. is a healthy, active 15-year-old. . . . The same cannot be said for most children in America with AD/HD. Every time [my son] sees one of these reports about AD/HD not existing and medication being a bad thing, he gets furious. He can't understand why people would talk that way about treatments that have helped him so much with a disorder that once left him virtually disabled.

Kingsley also points out another issue: the media always benefits when a controversy is created, and there is certainly a well-publicized controversy raging over Ritalin and ADHD.

Is Ritalin a controversial drug? Clearly. Can Ritalin be abused? Definitely. Should Ritalin be used carefully, with adequate supervision? Obviously. But should this drug be outlawed altogether? Not if people like Ellen Kingsley and Dr. Russell Barkley are correct in their opinion that Ritalin offers genuine medical help to individuals who experience a physical condition that is all too real.

If you have to make a decision about Ritalin—or any drug—it's important to get all the facts. Gather information about the drug's pros and cons. Read, check out reliable sites on the Internet, and talk to your doctor. Then you can make an informed decision, one that works for you and your family.

And remember, Ritalin is a medication for specific conditions. It was not developed to make you appear to be smarter or more hardworking. When abused, Ritalin brings with it a set of problems that will make you regret getting started down the path of artificial boosters—definitely a not-so-smart decision.

# Glossary

*amphetamines*: Central nervous system stimulants used to treat depression and as appetite suppressants.

*angina:* A medical condition in which a lack of blood to the heart causes severe chest pains.

*atomoxetine:* A selective norepinephrine reuptake inhibitor used in the treatment of ADHD.

*binges:* Short periods during which someone consumes far too much.

*chiropractic:* A medical system based on the theory that disease and disorders are caused by a misalignment of the bones, especially in the spine, that obstructs proper nerve functions.

*chronic:* Long-lasting or recurring frequently.

*clearinghouse:* An agency or organization that collects and distributes information.

*cognitive:* Relating to the process of acquiring knowledge through reasoning, intuition, or perception.

*compromise:* Expose to danger or disgrace.

*compulsive:* Driven by an irresistible inner force to do something.

*conditioned:* Made someone react in a certain way by gradually getting them used to a certain pattern of events.

*consensus:* General or widespread agreement among all members of a group.

*contraindicated:* Reasons why a medication should not be taken.

*emulating:* Imitating someone in order to equal or surpass the person.

*entrepreneurs:* People who assume the risk and responsibility of running a business.

**formication:** A neurologically based hallucination in which someone feels as though insects are crawling on her skin.

**glaucoma:** An eye disorder characterized by an abnormally high pressure in the eyeball.

**Hobson's choice:** An apparently free choice when there is no real alternative.

**impulsive:** Having the tendency to act on sudden urges or desires.

**monoamine oxidase inhibitor (MAOI):** An antidepressant that works by blocking the breakdown of monoamines in the brain.

**motor tics:** Sudden involuntary muscle contractions, especially of facial, neck, or shoulder muscles.

**mutations:** Random changes in a gene or chromosome resulting in a new trait or characteristic that can be inherited.

**narcolepsy:** A condition characterized by frequent, brief, and uncontrollable bouts of deep sleep, sometimes accompanied by hallucinations and an inability to move.

**off-label uses:** The use of medications for reasons other than for what they have received approval.

**palpitations:** Irregular or unusually rapid beating of the heart.

**patented:** Received exclusive rights from the government to make or sell an invention.

**pervasive:** Widespread.

**pharmacological:** Relating to drugs.

**Physicians' Desk Reference:** A book that contains the contents of the package inserts provided with prescription drugs.

**proactive:** Taking the initiative by acting rather than reacting to events.

**pseudoscience:** A theory or method doubtfully or mistakenly held to be scientific.

**psychoneuroses:** Mild psychiatric disorders characterized by anxiety and depression.

**relapse:** Revert to previous behavior.

**startle response:** The body's reaction to a sudden, unexpected stimulus.

**stimulants:** Drugs or other agents that produce a temporary increase in functional activity of a body organ or part.

**stroke:** Sudden loss of consciousness, sensation, and voluntary motion caused by a rupture or obstruction of a blood vessel in the brain.

**tachyarrhythmias:** Fast and irregular heartbeats.

**temporal:** Connected with life in the world, rather than spiritual life.

**thyrotoxicosis:** The overproduction of thyroid hormones at a dangerously high level; hyperthyroidism.

**Tourette's syndrome:** A condition in which someone experiences multiple tics and twitches, and utters involuntary grunts and obscene speech.

**toxic psychosis:** Psychotic symptoms associated with confusion, which usually occur after ingestion of large amounts of a substance by someone with no significant psychiatric history.

**traditional college students:** College students who are under twenty-four years of age and began attending college right after graduation from high school.

**transdermal:** Through the skin.

**twin studies:** A research method in which twins are used as subjects, with one serving as the control.

**vernacular:** The distinctive language or vocabulary of a particular profession, group, or class.

# Further Reading

Beal, Eileen J. *Ritalin*. New York: Rosen, 2003.

Breggin, Peter R. *The Ritalin Fact Book: What Your Doctor Won't Tell You About Stimulant Drugs*. Cambridge, Mass.: Perseus, 2002.

Brinkerhoff, Shirley. *Stuck on Fast Forward: Youth with Attention-Deficit/Hyperactivity Disorder*. Broomall, Pa.: Mason Crest, 2004.

Ferreiro, Carmen. *Ritalin and Other Methylphenidate-Containing Drugs*. New York: Chelsea House, 2006.

Menhard, Francha Roffe. *Facts About Ritalin*. New York: Benchmark Books, 2006.

Wurtzel, Elizabeth. *More, Now, Again: A Memoir of Addiction*. New York: Simon and Schuster, 2003.

# For More Information

ADHD Canada
www.adhdcanada.com

CHADD (Children and Adults with Attention Deficit/Hyperactivity Disorder)
www.chadd.org
www.chaddcanada.org (CHADD Canada)

Focus on ADHD
www.focusonadhd.com

Methylphenidate
www.mentalhealth.com/drug/p30-r03.html

Partnership for a Drug-Free America
www.drugfree.org

Ritalin Abuse
www.coolnurse.com/ritalin.htm

Ritalin Addiction
www.ritalinaddiction.com

Ritalin: Fast Facts
www.doitnow.org/pages/526.html

Ritalin Fast Facts: Questions and Answers
justice.gov/ndic/pubs6/6444/index.htm

The websites listed on this page were active at the time of publication. The publisher is not responsible for websites that have changed their addresses or discontinued operation since the date of publication. The publisher will review and update the website list upon each reprint.

# Bibliography

Barkley, Russell A. *Attention-Deficit Hyperactivity Disorder: A Handbook for Diagnosis and Treatment.* New York: Guilford Publications, 2006.

Barkley, Russell A. *Taking Charge of ADHD: The Complete Authoritative Guide for Parents.* New York: Guilford Publications, 2000.

Bussing, Regina. "Diagnosing ADHD/ADD in Children." Psych Central. http://psychcentral.com/library/adhd_diagchild.htm.

"FDA Approves Methylphenidate Patch to Treat Attention Deficit Hyperactivity Disorder in Children." FDA News, April 10, 2006. http://www.fda.gov/bbs/topics/NEWS/2006/NEW01352.html.

Gordon, Susan Merle, and Karen C. Adam. "Ritalin: Its Use and Abuse in Adults and Adolescents." *Paradigm* (Winter): 8–9.

"Health Canada Withdraws ADHD Drug." http://www.cbc.ca/story/science/national/2005/02.

Kapner, Daniel Ari. "Infofacts Resources: Recreational Use of Ritalin on College Campuses." Higher Education Center for Alcohol and Other Drug Abuse. http://www.higheredcenter.org/pubs/factsheets/ritalin.html.

Kozloff, Nicole. "Can I Have Your Attention, Please? Unprescribed Ritalin Use Popular With Frustrated Students." *McGill Daily*, March 21. 2005. http://www.mcgilldaily.com/view.php?aid=3853.

Kozloff, Nicole. "In Search of that Extra Edge." *The Gateway* 95, no. 5(July 2005). http://www.gateway.ualberta.ca/view.php?aid=4520.

"Methylphenidate." http://www.mentalhealth.com/drug/p30-r03.html.

Morton, W. Alexander, and Gwendolyn G. Stockton. "Methylphenidate Abuse and Psychiatric Side Effects." *Journal of Clinical Psychiatry* 2, no. 5(October 2000): 159–164.

National Institute of Drug Abuse. *NIDA InfoFacts: Methylphenidate (Ritalin).* Washington, D.C.: National Institutes of Health, U.S. Department of Health & Human Services, 2006.

"Quick Fix?" Health Talk@Mac 7, no. 4 (March 2004). http://www.mcmaster.ca/health/hwc/Newsletters/Mar04.html.

Richardson, Wendy. "AD/HD and Stimulant Medication Abuse." Attention Deficit Disorder Association. http://www.add.org/articles/med_abuse.html.

"Ritalin Alert: As Abuse Rates Climb, Schools Are Scrutinized." http://school.familyeducation.com.

"Ritalin Getting Into Wrong Hands: Survey." CBC.ca News, October 16, 2001. http://www.cbc.ca/story/news/national/2001/10/15/ritalin011015.html.

Stordy, B. Jacqueline, and Malcolm J. Nicholl. *The LCP Solution: The Remarkable Nutritional Treatment for ADHD, Dyslexia and Dyspraxia.* New York: Random House, 2000.

Sturino, Idella. "Student Abuse of Ritalin Raises Questions About Familiar Drug." *The Peak* 98, no. 7 (1998). http://www.sfu.ca/thepeak/98-1/issue7/ritalin.html.

Szuflita, Nick. "Ritalin Abuse Is Increasing." *Johns Hopkins News-Letter,* November 22, 2002. http://www.jhunewsletter.com.

"Teens Sell, Give Away Ritalin." *Connection,* December 2001. http://communications.medicine.dal.ca/archives/connection/dec2001.

"Trends in the Use of Ritalin in Canada." http://www.scienceblog.com/community/older/2001/B/200111573.html.

Virtue, Jeannine. "Ritalin (Methylphenidate) Drug Abuse." SelfGrowth.com. http://www.selfgrowth.com/articles/Virtue1.html.

Weihman, Ted. "Ritalin Abuse Graduates from College." Columbia News Service. http://www.jrn.columbia.edu/studentwork/cns/2003-03-14/62.asp.

# Index

# Picture Credits

Drug Enforcement Agency, p. 50
fotalia, p. 77
www.istock.com, pp. 13, 22, 59, 94, 110
        Paul Cowan, p. 110
        James Goldsworthy, p. 13
        Nancy Louie, p. 78
        Michelle Malven, p. 94
        Chris Schmidt, p. 22
Tyler Stalman, p. 59
Jupiter Images, pp. 10,17, 20, 25, 29, 31, 32, 34, 36, 39, 41, 43, 44,
46, 52, 54, 57, 60, 64, 72, 75, 82, 84, 87, 90, 93, 98, 100, 102, 105,
109, 113, 114
Laurley, p. 8
Malinda Miller, p. 15
Photodisc, p. 35

To the best knowledge of the publisher, all other images are in the
public domain. If any image has been inadvertently uncredited,
please notify Harding House Publishing Services, Vestal, New York
13850, so that rectification can be made for future printings.

# Author and Consultant Biographies

## Author

Ida Walker is a graduate of the University of Northern Iowa in Cedar Falls, and has done graduate work at Syracuse University. The author of several nonfiction books, she currently lives in Upstate New York.

## Series Consultant

Jack E. Henningfield, Ph.D., is a professor at the Johns Hopkins University School of Medicine, and he is also Vice President for Research and Health Policy at Pinney Associates, a consulting firm in Bethesda, Maryland, that specializes in science policy and regulatory issues concerning public health, medications development, and behavior-focused disease management. Dr. Henningfield has contributed information relating to addiction to numerous reports of the U.S. Surgeon General, the National Academy of Sciences, and the World Health Organization.